AF392390

The Five Steps
To
Purify
Your Soul

OMER SULAYMAN

In the Name of Allaah, The Most Merciful, The
Bestower of Mercy

Table of Contents

Introduction

All praise is due to Allah. We praise Him, seek His help and forgiveness, and we seek refuge in Him from the evil of our souls and our misdeeds.

I bear witness that there is no deity worthy of worship except Allah alone. He has no partner. I also bear witness that Muhammad (peace and blessings of Allah be upon him) is His slave and messenger.

This book is based on the teachings of Imam Ibn Al-Qayyim Al-Jawziyah, Imam Ibn Rajab Al Hanbali, Imam Ibn Taymiyyah, Imam Ibn Qudamah Al-Maqdisi, and Shaykh Abdur-Razzaq-al-Badr. It explains in detail how to purify the soul, heal the heart, and remove heart (spiritual) diseases according to the Qur'an and Sunnah

New Muslims and beginners are eager to know the purification process in Islam. I hope this book will fulfill this purpose and help them understand this beautiful process to purify their soul and their heart.

Everyone is made of three essential components - the body, the soul and the intellect. They all work together to give us our character. The soul or *'nafs'* is the most important thing.

You should be concerned about the health and well-being of your soul just as you are concerned about the health of your body. The soul has requirements that it needs to make it healthy. We should not neglect them, or we will suffer from diseases of the heart (not the physical heart, but the spiritual heart).

The purification of the soul in Arabic is called *tazkiyyah*. It sounds like *zakah* (obligatory charity). In the same way that we purify our wealth and increase it when we give *zakah*, *tazkiyyah takes* care of the *nafs* (soul), purifying it and cleansing it. We cleanse our soul from heart diseases and bad qualities. With *tazkiyyah* our souls grow in status and closeness to Allah.

The origin of the word *'Tazkiyah'* is from a word that has the meaning of 'development' or 'to increase and become more in number'. It refers to developing the soul, fixing it with exalted qualities, noble manners and righteous actions.

Tazkiyah increases the good deeds and praiseworthy qualities of the soul. A person who wants to purify his soul should protect it from unworthy traits and despicable character.

Our journey in this world is a trial and our success lies in returning to *Jannah* (Paradise). Every day we struggle to clean up our soul and get better is a day well spent. It is a day that was profitable. If we cleanse and purify our soul every day, it will lead to our success in the hereafter. Our hearts often become rusty and need to be cleaned again and again. With purification you learn how to renew your *Iman* (faith). With the purification of the soul, you will taste the sweetness of faith.

Purification of the soul should be our main concern. This is not an ordinary task. We must purify our souls and pay attention to this purification process. This is critical as spiritual diseases can destroy us. So we have to take care of them and treat them. It is important to study the purification of the soul and know how to do it. It is important to control the soul.

The soul or *nafs* is like a mount or a horse. It's like a wild animal. If a person does not have control over the mount, he will not be able to travel on it. The beast will take him where it will. But if the person takes control of the animal, trains it, then this animal will know who is the owner and will obey him. Similarly, if a person does not train his soul, he will follow his *nafs* and do the evil deeds that the soul desires. He becomes the slave of the soul, and the soul becomes his master. But if he trains his soul and refuses to obey every whim and demand of the soul, then he will keep his soul in check and this will lead him to paradise.

Imam Hasan al-Basri (may Allah have mercy on him) said: *"The nafs is like a strong horse. The goal is not to kill it but to tame it. It is good if you have a strong and powerful horse, but you must have control over it, and not the other way around."*

Allah took eleven oaths in the Quran before saying that the successful are those who purify their souls. Allah swears to emphasize the seriousness of something, and in this case it is the fact that the person who purifies his soul is successful. The burden of purification is upon us, and we should make an effort to purify ourselves and be among those who succeed.

We should pray to Allah to help us in this purification.

Allah purifies us in many ways. One of the ways is by testing us. Allah allows a person to struggle and go through some hardship to cleanse him from sins. The Prophet (peace and blessings of Allah be upon him) said: *"Allah will continue to test the believer or try them until he cleanses them of all his sins, until he meets Allah like a newborn baby."*

Someone may ask, 'Why can't I benefit from the Qur'an? Why can't I wake up for morning prayer? Why is everyone else in the mosque crying except me?' It is because of our sins that our hearts are eaten away and we do not find peace and enjoyment in our worship. The heart is made to naturally love Allah and obey Him, but sins prevent it from realizing this potential.

It is obligatory for us to purify our soul.

At the moment of death, there is a sudden change in currency. All the dollars or dirhams you have in your pocket will become worthless. The only things that matter after death are your correct beliefs, good deeds, and sound heart. Success in the hereafter depends on the conditions in our hearts that we carry with us. On the Day of Judgment, neither wealth nor children will be of any use. Only those who come before Allah with a pure heart will be saved.

To cleanse our souls, we should recognize the diseases that harm our souls. After recognition we should get rid of these diseases. Along with this treatment, we should decorate our soul with the qualities that give it strength. So, to purify our souls, we should worship Allah based on the Qur'an and Sunnah, remove our bad qualities, treat heart diseases when they are present, and acquire good qualities. For example, if your soul is a garden, in order for it to be fruitful and grow beneficial plants, you should first remove the weeds (heart disease and the bad qualities). Later, you need to use fertilizers, which are the good properties to further purify your soul. Along with this you should increase your worship of Allah.

Ibadah (worship) is a comprehensive word meaning a state of submission and humility to Allah. It is combined with absolute love and worship of Allah. Worship includes all words, actions and avoidance of bad things that we do to please Allah.

We should concentrate both on improving the society and also the purification of our soul. We should not neglect ourselves when we invite others to Islam and the truth. Allah says in the Qur'an: *"Save yourself and your family from the Fire."* Although we are concerned about society, we should save ourselves first.

When we learn about the purification of the soul, we should have the intention that we will act on this knowledge and strive to purify our souls. Action should accompany knowledge. We should obey Allah and hope for success. Success is having a purified soul. This knowledge of purification of the soul is for you first and later after learning and practicing you should share it with others.

Allah has rights over you, your family has rights over you, and your soul and body have rights over you. You should fulfill all these rights. You should not be in the mosque all the time so that you neglect your family. You should fulfill your family duties and also purify your soul as much as possible. You don't have to leave your house and go somewhere to cleanse your soul. You can purify your soul even when you are with your family. You don't have to become a monk or go to the hill or monasteries to purify yourself. You should not avoid getting married or having children in order to purify yourself. You should be a good man and take care of your wife and children while you purify your soul. Taking care of your family to please Allah is part of the worship of Allah that purifies your soul.

We should know the goal of purification. Before we begin a purification path or course, we need to know the goal it seeks to achieve. Our goal of purification is to worship and please Allah completely and properly, and to become a truthful servant of Allah.

This goal is achieved by strengthening one's faith and humbly submitting to Allah through obligatory and voluntary actions. Both outward submission and submission of the soul are required to achieve this goal. You should perform all the mandatory actions. Along with this, you should do the recommended actions as much as possible.

We must educate ourselves to know what Allah and His Messenger have taught us and the actions that please them. We should be happy to perform these actions regularly and properly. We should not do the actions which were not taught by the Prophet (peace and blessings be upon him) as these will not purify our souls. The way to worship Allah has been taught to us by Him and we should not worship Him based on our inclinations, logic or whims. To purify our soul, we should only follow the Quran and authentic narrations from the Prophet and not follow the newly invented actions.

Allah says in the Qur'an,

"Say: Are those who know equal to those who do not know? Only they will remember (who are) people of understanding."

Allah wants us to seek knowledge and be with people of knowledge. Allah exalts the people of knowledge with the correct faith among mankind. Knowledge affects our spiritual cleansing process and we need to acquire authentic knowledge on how to cleanse our soul.

The Prophet said: *"Whoever does not acquire knowledge solely with the intention of seeking the pleasure of Allah, but for worldly gain, will not smell the fragrance of Paradise on the Day of Resurrection."* The purpose of seeking knowledge should be to purify our own soul and not to make money or become famous.

We should implement knowledge after learning it. We should recognize these teachings of the Qur'an and Sunnah as the truly good things that Allah has blessed us with. We should love them and act on them. Just knowing will not guide a person if he does not act in accordance with his knowledge.

For our worship to be beneficial to us, we must make sure that we worship Allah sincerely to please Him and for His sake. Our worship should be in accordance with what Allah has revealed in the Qur'an and Sunnah.

Our actions must be sincere and also correct. An act done sincerely but not correctly is not accepted. When done correctly but not sincerely, it is again not accepted. So for our worship to be accepted, it should be both sincere and correct. It must be according to the Qur'an and Sunnah. We should worship Allah with an utmost degree of love for Him. None other than Allah deserves our total love, obedience and submission.

If your heart is purified, it will be reflected in your actions. Your prayers will improve. You will begin to pray more and will also perform the recommended actions such as fasting regularly. You will develop many good and commendable qualities such as truthfulness and honesty. You become a helpful person and have empathy for others.

Purification is a continuous process that only ends with our death. There is no level or point in our life beyond which purification is not required. Purifying our soul is a continuous struggle and we always need to perform ritual acts of worship and other purifying acts.

Ibadah or worship is not limited to the ritual acts of worship, but this is a comprehensive term that includes all our daily actions when performed to please Allah. So we have to purify all our actions and do them with the correct intention to please Allah and live the honorable life as a servant of Allah. All our daily routines become acts of purification when performed with the correct intention of worshiping Allah. Purification of the soul is a comprehensive and all-encompassing process that affects all aspects of our lives.

There are many actions one can take to purify the soul. However, the path is only one – Islam – submission to Allah and following the Qur'an and Sunnah.

A new way or *dhikr* (remembrance) that is not based on the Qur'an or Sunnah will not bring a person closer to Allah. You should stick to what Allah and His Messenger have taught. Newly invented actions will only make a person closer to Satan.

Knowledge of purification is available to everyone. This is easily found in the Qur'an and Sunnah and anyone can access it. It is not a hidden secret or a mystery.

Purification develops your soul and refines character. It removes the bad aspects of your character and treats the diseases of the spiritual heart. With purification, you will understand your life's purpose and goal. You will know how to live your life in a way that is pleasing to your Creator. You will experience true happiness when you purify your soul.

Learning the truth from the Qur'an and Sunnah is the first component of purification. This will purify your faith. The next step would be to get closer to Allah by the obligatory acts. After this would be to get even closer to Allah by voluntary actions. The heart does not become pure until it obtains what benefits it (the right beliefs, righteous actions, and good qualities) and suppresses what harms it (the wrong beliefs, evil actions, heart diseases, and bad qualities).

You will succeed in purifying your soul as long as you strive to become a better Muslim. You will succeed because Allah will help, bless and guide you to become a better Muslim.

Step 1: Purification of Faith

Tawheed

Your faith and belief are the most important. You act on what you believe. You don't do things that you think are wrong, but do things that you think are right. If you believe that you have a Creator who will hold you accountable for your actions, you will avoid actions that will harm you in the Hereafter. Your beliefs and faith are the first things that Allah will judge on the Day of Judgment. If your faith in the One True God is lacking, your good works will be of no use. So the first step in purification is the purification of faith. Only if your beliefs are correct and according to the Qur'an and Sunnah, your actions will purify you further.

Tawheed (correct belief and worship of Allah alone) is the most important aspect of purifying your soul. Allah says in the Qur'an,

'He who has purified himself has certainly succeeded.'

Allah praises the one who tries to purify himself, and this verse refers to those who purified themselves from *shirk* (associating partners with Allah) and *kufr* (disbelief). Without worshiping our Creator as He wants us to worship Him, we can never purify ourselves by any other action. Only after worshiping Him correctly, further acts of purification help us become better Muslims. Any action that is not done with the correct intention of doing it purely and solely for the sake of Allah will be rejected and will not help us purify our souls.

Tawheed is the basis of the purification of the soul. The foundation is the most important structure of the building. If it is strong, whatever you build on it will also be strong and will last a long time. If the foundation is weak, then no matter how strong you build something on it - it will not be strong and will not last for a long time. If *Tawheed* is not in order, then all your good deeds will not be beneficial and will not purify your soul. Actions in Islam have no value unless they are built on *Tawheed*.

Tawheed is important because humans were created for this. It is the purpose of our creation and existence. Muslims should strive to achieve this goal and worship Allah alone as He deserves to be worshipped. Allah says in the Qur'an,

'I have not created the jinn and men except to worship Me (alone)'.

Whoever does not fulfill the reason for his creation (to worship only Allah) has wasted his life. *Tawheed* is the reason Messengers were sent by Allah and His Books were revealed.

We worship Allah because He alone deserves our worship. Allah does not need our worship and we worship Him to serve our own interest and well-being in this life and the Hereafter.

The main message of the prophets and messengers was *Tawheed*. Only worshiping Allah purifies the soul. *Tawheed* purifies our hearts by removing the worship of everything other than Allah from the heart, and it confirms the worship of Allah alone. *Shirk* (worship and asking help from other than Allah such as asking help from dead people or grave worship) pollutes our souls and through *Shirk* a person loses all his good deeds. Worshiping anything other than Allah corrupts the heart and makes it sick. *Tawheed* purifies our hearts and keeps them healthy. There is no purification of the soul unless we completely free ourselves from *shirk* in all its types - major *shirk*, minor *shirk*,

shirk in intention, speech and action. We should free ourselves from everything that contradicts *Tawheed* if we want to purify our hearts and souls.

We should perform all acts of worship only for the sake of Allah. We should be sincere and our intention should be free from all impurities if we want to get closer to Allah. The intention behind all acts of worship should be to obtain only the pleasure of Allah. Allah says in the Qur'an, *'And they have been commanded to worship only Allah, being sincere to Him in their religion..."*

Having the intention of being praised by the people when doing a good deed is a wrong and evil intention that will not help us to purify our soul. A person can prolong his prayer if someone is watching him, and this prolongation of the prayer will not benefit him, as it was not done for the pleasure of Allah. When you do good righteous deeds so that others may admire you, you are acting for their admiration and not for the pleasure of Allah. Our intentions and our actions should be pure. Only then will they purify our souls.

The heart is the place of our intentions. It's not the lips. The Prophet (peace and blessings of Allah be upon him) said: *'Deeds are judged according to the intention'.* If our heart is pure, our intentions will also be pure. This will make our deeds correct and pure.

You should avoid telling others about your good deeds if it is of no benefit to them. You should hide your good deeds and this will be a proof that you did it only to please Allah. In this way your heart will be purified.

You should not be proud of yourself when you do good deeds. You did the good deeds only because Allah wanted you to do them. You could not have done them without the help of Allah. You should thank Allah and praise Him for allowing you to do the good deed and for enabling you to do it.

A person can never purify himself if he associates partners with Allah. The greatest wrong and evil act is associating a partner with Allah, and after doing this impure act it is not possible to become pure by any other act.

Allah says in the Qur'an, *'O believers! Indeed, the polytheists are impure.'*

Tawheed is the foundation of purification and all other good deeds are built on it. We should thank Allah for guiding us to worship Him and purifying our hearts.

Allah says in the Qur'an, *'And had it not been for Allah's Grace and His Mercy upon you, none of you would ever have been clean of sins...'*

We should be grateful to Allah for purifying us. We are not entitled to the things and blessings that Allah has given us. Allah does not owe us anything and it is only from His mercy that we are blessed and purified. This is a favor from Allah, even if we disobey. So we should never be ungrateful to Allah and we should always thank Him for His blessings and favors.

Follow the way of the Prophet (peace and blessings be upon him)

We should follow the path of the Prophet to increase our faith in Allah. No one is more knowledgeable about Allah or has greater fear of Him than the Prophet.

We should know the names of Allah, their meanings and act upon them.

The Prophet has taught us this knowledge. Allah sent him for this purpose and we should follow him and imitate him to purify our souls.

Allah says in the Qur'an, *'Say (O Muhammad): If you love Allah, follow me. Allah will love you.'*

The Prophet is the 'Example' for us and everyone until the Day of Judgment. The knowledge of his (peace and blessings of Allah be upon him) wonderful life demonstrates to us the right and only method of purification. To purify ourselves, we must love the Prophet until he is loved by us more than all mankind.

To know the way of the Prophet, you should study the words of the Prophet and learn more about his blessed life. You should consider the lessons you can learn from his life and act on that knowledge.

We should take the Prophet as our role model and as an example to follow on this path to the purification of our souls.

Allah says in the Qur'an, *'Verily in the Messenger of Allah you have a good example to follow, for him who hopes for (the meeting with) Allah and the Last Day'*.

We should take the Messenger as an example in his speech and actions. It is not possible to purify the souls except by following the Messenger.

Allah says in the Qur'an, *'Say (O Muhammad): If you love Allah, then follow me, Allah will love you and forgive you your sins. And Allah is Forgiving, Most Merciful'*.

If we love the Prophet and want to purify our souls, then we should follow the Prophet. Any action that does not have any proof or any basis from the Book of Allah and the Sunnah of His Prophet can never purify your soul. The only thing that leads to the purification of souls is following the Messenger.

The Prophet (peace and blessings of Allah be upon him) said: *'Everyone in my Ummah (nation) will enter Paradise except those who refuse.'* He was asked: *'Who will refuse?'* He (peace and blessings be upon him) said: *'Whoever obeys me shall enter Paradise, and whoever disobeys me has refused (to enter Paradise.)'*

Other Beliefs That Help Purify Our Soul

A correct belief in the angels, the books of Allah, destiny and the hereafter will guide us towards the purification of our soul. Read a good book such as *Explanation of Shaikh Al-Islam Ibn Taymiyyah's Al-Aqidah Al-Wasitiyyah by the virtuous Sheikh Muhammad bin Salih Al-Uthaimeen (may Allah have mercy upon them)* to learn the correct beliefs.

We feel blessed to be Muslims when we have a firm belief in Islam. Believing in all the pillars of faith encourages us to do as many good deeds as possible. We avoid sins knowing that angels are watching over us. We are responsible for our actions and must answer for them in the hereafter. This belief keeps our desires in check.

Allah knows what we do and what is in our hearts. If your beliefs are correct your actions will be correct. With the correct faith, you will realize that the obligatory prayers and many actions in Islam are obligatory and cannot be abandoned by a Muslim. Faith is composed of the belief of the heart, the speech of the tongue, and the actions of the body.

When we do good deeds after having the correct belief, we are blessed with Allah's mercy. With Allah's grace we can enter paradise. Without righteous actions, even if we have the correct beliefs, we may not deserve Allah's mercy.

Allah says in many places in the Qur'an that only those who believe and do righteous deeds will be rewarded. It is faith combined with good deeds that separates Muslims from others.

Allah says in the Qur'an: *'Whoever hopes to meet his Lord, let him work righteously, and in the worship of his Lord admit no one as a partner.'*

Step 2: Treatment of heart disease and removal of bad qualities

Types of hearts and souls

A person who wants good for himself and who wants to purify his soul should understand the qualities and actions of the pure soul so that his soul can be like that. He should be careful and not do what the corrupt soul asks him to do.

The pure souls are satisfied only with the best and loftiest causes that have the most praiseworthy results. The corrupt souls concentrate on lowly dirty matters and fall upon it like a fly upon dirt. The noble soul is not satisfied with oppression, obscenity, theft and deceit, for it is above all these. The corrupt soul prefers oppression, obscenity, theft and deceit.

Hearts are of three types. The real alive and correct heart, the dead heart and the defective heart.

The correct heart is that which is secured from all desires that oppose Allah's command. It is secured from any doubt about His commands and His prohibitions. It worships none but Allah and follows none but the teachings of His Prophet. This is the living, humble, soft and gentle heart.

A dead heart contains no life - it does not know its Lord and does not worship Him. This is the dry, dirty, hardened and dead heart.

A defective heart lives but is defective. It is alive because it loves Allah, believes in Him, is sincere and trusts in Him. But it also loves vain desires and gives them preference. This makes the heart defective. It oscillates between being alive and being defective. This is the diseased heart that can move towards becoming a proper heart if the disease is treated and cured. But it can also progress towards death if the heart disease is uncontrolled and takes complete control of the heart. The living heart and its enlightenment is the cause of all good, while the dead heart and its darkness is the cause of all evil that exists within it.The heart can only be alive and correct when we realize the truth, love it and prefer it above all else.

The main cause of heart disease is wishful thinking and doubt. The heart can never find happiness unless it makes Allah its sole object of worship and desire.

We can perfect the heart and purify it by repentance and by forsaking all forms of false love and contemptible characteristics. A person should strive hard against his soul that incites evil and hold fast to Allah. He should fight *the satans* among the *jinn* and men by knowing their plans and goals. He should protect himself from them through the remembrance of Allah and seek refuge with Him from them.

Ibn Taymiyyah (Allah be pleased with him) said, "When the dog barks at you and wants to attack you, do not fight the dog. Instead, tell the shepherd and ask him for help in controlling the dog. This will save you from trouble (with having to fight the dog)."

Similarly, if we want to fight our enemy Shaitaan, instead of fighting with him ourselves, we should seek refuge with Allah from Shaitaan. By doing this we will achieve success against our sworn enemy.

The Prophet (peace and blessings of Allah be upon him) said: *'There is a lump of flesh in the body – if it becomes good, the whole body becomes good, and if it becomes bad, the whole body becomes bad. And it is truly the heart'.* If the heart is good, it makes use of knowledge and acts on it. It avoids the forbidden and performs the recommended actions. If the heart is bad, then knowledge does not benefit it, and it follows its desires and indulges in what is forbidden. The heart is the part of the body that Allah has favored above all other parts. It is the place where *Tawheed* and *Iman* (faith) reside.

Heart poison

All acts of disobedience to Allah poison the heart and make it sick. The most common poisons in the heart are unnecessary talk, unrestrained glances, too much food and bad company.

The Prophet (peace and blessings of Allah be upon him) said: *'A servant's faith is not corrected until his heart is corrected, and his heart is not corrected until his tongue is corrected'.*

The purification of our souls is dependent on the purification of our hearts, and the purification of our hearts is dependent on the purification of our tongues.

Ibn Umar (Allah be pleased with him) said: *'Do not talk excessively without remembering Allah, because such excessive talk without mentioning Allah hardens the heart, and the person furthest from Allah is a person with a hard heart'.*

To purify yourself, speak only when necessary and only what benefits others.

Umar (Allah be pleased with him) said: *'A person who talks too much is a person who often makes mistakes, and a person who often makes mistakes often has wrong actions. The fire has priority over such a frequent sinner'.*

Argument to show your knowledge and defeat others is the source of evil. It leads to pride, which is a disease of the heart.

The Prophet (peace and blessings of Allah be upon him) said: *'Let anyone who believes in Allah and the Last Day either speak well or remain silent'.*

The speech that reminds others of good deeds and Allah - is praiseworthy and encouraging.

But idle chatter without benefit should be avoided.

The forbidden gaze can attract a person and this results in the image of what he saw being imprinted in his heart. This destroys the heart.

The Prophet (peace and blessings of Allah be upon him) said: 'The *gaze is a poisoned arrow from Satan. Whoever lowers his gaze before Allah, He will grant him a refreshing sweetness that he will find in his heart on the day he meets Him.*'

Satan enters the heart with the forbidden look that you should not see. Satan then corrupts the heart and poisons it. He makes what you saw look more beautiful than it is and tempts you to do more acts of disobedience. So avoid looking as it prevents further sins and keeps your heart clean and pure. If you lower your gaze for Allah, He will give you inner vision with abundant pure light.

When you eat small amounts of food, your heart is tender, your intellect is strong, and you are humble. With minimal food intake, your desire to sin is weak. But with excessive food intake, you will feel an increased urge to sin and disobey Allah. Excessive eating makes worship and obedience to Allah seem difficult. We can limit Satan's ways by eating less and by fasting.

When we remove the toxins and poisons from our hearts and souls, we will naturally lean towards Allah.

Satan's traps

We should know Satan's traps and his evil ways to avoid falling into them and destroying our souls. We will walk away and be careful only when we know there is a trap ahead.

Satan or *Iblis* comes to us as a counselor and shows false concern for us. He will lie and mislead you by telling you that he cares for you. He is a deceitful liar who should never be trusted.

Even when we recognize our sin, he further deceives us and advises us to continue sinning and not repent.

Satan's first trap is polytheism and unbelief. If he makes one person fall into this trap, his work is done. This is his ultimate goal - to make everyone fall into kufr and shirk. He tries hard to convince a person to associate partners with Allah and corrupt his soul. If he gives up hope of deceiving him with the first trap, he tries his next trap.

The second trap is innovation or *Bidah.*

The Prophet (peace and blessings of Allah be upon him) said: *'The worst is the newly invented matters (Bidah) in religion, and every newly invented matter in religion is an innovation, and every innovation is a misguidance, and every misguidance is in the fire of hell."*

So the sin of *Bidah* or a newly invented matter in religion is evil and is a trap of Satan. With innovation, Satan decorates something that is evil and makes it look good.

The Prophet (peace and blessings of Allah be upon him) said: *'Whoever introduces that which is not from (it – that is Islam), in this affair of ours, (then) it will be rejected'.*

When we purify our souls, we cannot purify them with a new act or *Bidah* (with something that was not taught by Allah and His Messenger), but we should purify our souls with the *Sunnah*. We should not fall into this trap of Satan.

Imam al-Sufyan al-Thawri (may Allah have mercy on him) said: "*A person of innovation never repents because he thinks it is good.*" Satan makes him do actions that are not from Allah and not from the *Sunnah*, but makes him think that it is a way to get closer to Allah.

Ibn Mas'ud (Allah be pleased with him) found people in the mosque sitting in a circle saying the remembrance of Allah with stones. He threw the stones at them and asked them the reason for using the stones as this has not been taught by the Prophet (peace and blessings of Allah be upon him). This was a new act and not from the Qur'an or the actions of the Prophet.

They said, "We only wanted to do good."

Ibn Mas'ud said: "*How many people desire good and never achieve it? If you do not stop this, then you will be the enemies of Allah.*"

The narrator of this incident said that these people were the first to join the *Khawarij* (a deviant group). Make sure that what you do is correct and based on the teachings of the Qur'an and Sunnah.

Satan's third trap is to try to get a person to commit a great sin. Iblis is eager to make a person commit a great sin in order to blacken his heart. For example, disobedience to parents is a great sin that Satan encourages a person to do to corrupt his soul. If we want to purify our souls and prevent them from becoming impure, then we should avoid major sins.

We should never commit a major sin, but if we have already done so, we should pray for repentance. Allah loves to forgive His servants when they repent. We should never lose hope in Allah and we should continue to purify our souls with repentance and good deeds. Iblis wants us to despair of Allah's mercy. We should not believe in Satan but return to Allah after committing the sin and repent.

Satan's fourth trap is the minor (lesser) sins trap. The lesser sins are like little sticks that people gather to light a fire. Each stick will only cause a small fire, but when gathered together, these small sticks will cause a huge fire. Minor sins add up and can destroy a person's soul and destroy him.

If Iblis fails to catch the person in this fourth trap of minor sins, he moves on to the next level.

The fifth trap is keeping a person busy with permissible actions (which don't earn him a reward and keep him away from doing rewardable actions). These permissible actions do not help the person to get a reward or cause him to be punished in the Hereafter. But by doing these permissible things, the person misses out on spending the time to do recommended things and obtain reward from Allah. His soul will not be purified if he is preoccupied with permissible things and misses doing beneficial actions.

If Satan fails at this level and is unable to make a person preoccupied with permissible actions, he moves on to the sixth level. He tries to occupy his time with good deeds which are not very rewarding. This person could have done very virtuous and rewarding good deeds, but Satan tries to make him do good deeds that are not very virtuous. So this person loses out on getting more rewards.

Satan orders a person to perform actions with fewer rewards. To purify our soul, we should be very careful in prioritizing our actions and should always perform more rewarding actions. We should spend our time in such a way that we get the most rewards. So always prioritize the actions and deeds that are most rewarding and do them more than other actions.

You should not miss out on the highly rewarding mandatory actions (obligatory deeds) to perform less rewarding voluntary actions. You should not miss praying the Fajr prayer because you prayed voluntary prayers throughout the night. If you do this, you will fall into Satan's sixth trap.

When the Prophet (peace and blessings be upon him) was asked which deeds are the most beloved and virtuous to Allah, he said: *'Prayer in time'*. When he was asked after that which deed was most loved by Allah, the Prophet replied: *'Kindness to parents.'*

You should keep fighting to purify your soul and be aware of these traps of Satan. Don't fall into any of these traps if you want to cleanse your soul and enter paradise. Purification is achieved only by performing good deeds and by avoiding evil deeds and satanic traps.

Allah says in the Qur'an, '*Verily, (with) My slaves you (Satan) have no power over them, except for those who willingly follow you*'.

Satan is the enemy of man. He will do anything to prevent us from purifying our souls.

The Prophet (peace and blessings of Allah be upon him) said: '*Satan puts obstacles in every way the son of Adam undertakes to obey Allah*'.

Hasan al-Basri (may Allah have mercy on him) said: '*If Satan sees you consistently obeying Allah, he will seek you again and again. If Satan sees that he is getting nowhere with you, he will eventually tire of you and reject you. But if a person keeps going back and forth (doing good deeds as well as sins), Satan continues to have hope (to catch him and take him to hell)*'.

We should fill our hearts with the love of Allah. Ibn al-Qayyim (Allah have mercy on him) said: '*The mind is like a mill, as long as you have useful grain inside it, nothing else can enter.*'

Satan can only influence us when Allah is not enough for us.

Allah says in the Qur'an: *'Is Allah not enough for him?'*

When Allah is enough for us, Satan cannot influence us. Only when we become careless and do not remember Allah, Satan can whisper to us.

The effect of sins on purity of heart

A sinner finds darkness in his heart. He feels in his heart the darkness of a pitch-black night. For every sin that a sinner commits, he has oppressed himself and his heart. He has not been fair to his heart and makes it suffer because of the sins. Because of his sins, he is the oppressor and the oppressed at the same time.

Like physical darkness in his eyes, when he commits sins, his heart darkens. Allah's obedience is light, while His disobedience leads to darkness. Each time he sins, the darkness intensifies, his confusion increases and misleads him further. He does not realize that sins darken his heart, just as a blind person does not realize the darkness of the night. If a person performs an action, he will receive the fruits of it, whether bitter or sweet. Sins result in bitter fruit. Staying away from sins results in sweet fruit.

Allah says in the Qur'an, *'He has the reward for what (good) he has earned, and he is punished for what (evil) he has earned...'*

Some of the Companions said: *'Verily good deeds are a light in the heart, strengthening the body, a glow in the face, a cause of abundant provision and love in the hearts of creation. Indeed, evil actions are darkness in the heart, a blackness in the face, a weakness of the body, a cause of the decrease of provisions and hatred in the hearts of creation.'*

An evil effect of sins is the weakening of the sinner's body and heart. With continued sins, his heart becomes completely weak and lifeless. The heart is dead, although it continues to beat physically. The life of *Iman* (faith) is the true life of the heart.

The Prophet (peace and blessings of Allah be upon him) said: *'Verily, in the body is a piece of flesh. If it stands upright, the rest of the body will stand upright. If it is corrupt, the rest of the body will be corrupt. Yes, (this piece of flesh) is the heart'.*

All actions affect the heart. Beneficial actions purify the heart. Sinful actions damage the heart. The good and beneficial actions constitute righteousness for the soul and heart, whereas the bad actions oppress the soul and heart.

Allah says in the Qur'an: *'Whoever does righteous deeds, it is for his own benefit, and whoever does evil, it is against his own self.'*

Allah says in the Qur'an, *'No! But in their hearts is the Raan (covering of sins and evil deeds) which they used to serve'*. This is from committing one sin after another.

Al-Hasan Al-Basri (Allah have mercy on him) said: *'This is one sin after another until it blinds the heart.'* The heart wears away because of sins. The living lighted heart hears, sees and understands, because of the light it contains, while the dead heart does not hear, see, or understand.

If our sins increase, then the corrosion in the heart also increases until it gets covered by *'Raan'*. Afterwards it is sealed and locked. At this stage his enemy, Satan, makes his advances and can drive him wherever he wants.

The Prophet (peace and blessings of Allah be upon him) said: '*When the believer commits a sin, a black spot appears on his heart. If he repents and forsakes that sin and seeks forgiveness, his heart will be polished. But if (the sin) increases, (the black spot) increases until it takes over the heart. It's Raan.*'

But if that person remembers Allah and turns to Him, the heart is polished again. We should ask Allah to protect our hearts and our bodies and keep us away from sins.

Sins reduce the determination of the heart to repent and purify itself. This is one of the most terrible evil effects of sin. Sins weaken the heart and reduce its willingness to repent. As the resolve and desire to sin is strengthened, the will to repent of sin diminishes with continued sins until it is completely removed from the sinner's heart.

The heart becomes so addicted to sin that even though he outwardly repents with his tongue, his heart is bound to sin. He is persistent in sinning and determined to sin whenever he can.

This is a great disease of the heart and leads to the destruction of the sinner.

The resolve to do good and repent is weakened because of the sins. Before committing sins, a person has a strong will in his heart for good deeds. But sins reduce this determination and increase the will to do bad actions.

Before a person falls into sin, his soul is reluctant to sin. Although he approached the sin, his soul fears to commit it. But after he entered into it and committed the sin and continues to commit it, his soul no longer feels restrained and his heart continues to weaken.

The Prophet (peace and blessings of Allah be upon him) said: *'Allah has set an example of the straight path. On both sides of the path are two walls, on the two walls are open doors and on the open doors are curtains. There is one who calls at the beginning of the road saying – O slaves of Allah! Enter the path and do not deviate from it. Meanwhile, a caller from the middle of the path said - O slave of Allah! Don't open it, because if you open it, you'll go in'.*

The straight path is Islam, and the two walls are Allah's appointed boundaries. The doors with the curtains are Allah's prohibition. The one who calls at the beginning of the path is the Qur'an - the book of Allah. The caller in the middle of the path is the heart of every Muslim who gives a warning from Allah. When you enter the door in the middle of the path, it will be difficult for you to get out of it.

If you open the door to sin, you will find in your heart pain, tightness and discomfort. If someone or something invites a righteous person to disobey Allah, then he feels uncomfortable. But if he was overcome because of the invitation of the people of evil, or because his soul was inclined to evil, or because of Satan, then he enters the path of sin, and he crosses this path for a long time - leading to weakening of warnings that his heart is giving out until there is no more warning and his heart dies.

The heart weakens until the desire to repent is completely removed. When a person is on the path of sin, his heart and soul continue to advise him to repent. But if the path of sin is prolonged, one day he will reach a station where the desire to repent is completely removed and he will not even think of repenting.

Even if half of this decision to repent dies because of sins, then he will not repent to Allah because the sin would be deeply embedded in his heart.

Abstaining from indecent acts and sins leads to purification of the heart. When one forsakes bad actions and repents of sin, the heart is purified and freed from pollution. When a person sins, the heart becomes weak because of the mixture of righteous actions with evil actions. So when a person leaves the sinful actions and repents, the heart becomes strong and it is eager to perform righteous actions.

You should ask yourself, 'What is there between me and Allah that prevents me from being purified? What prevents my soul from getting closer to Allah? What prevents me from having a soul that is at peace?' Once you answer these questions and get rid of these bad qualities and heart diseases, you will naturally come closer to Allah with a pure heart.

You should close all the ways that lead to sin. Closing the paths of evil is extremely important to purify the soul. When you go towards Allah and seek to purify to save your soul, you will find many paths that take you away from purifying your soul.

The Prophet (peace and blessings of Allah be upon him) said: *'Indeed, Allah sets forth an example of the straight path, and on its two sides are two walls'*. Imagine this example. You are walking on a straight road and to your left is a wall and to your right is a wall. On the two walls, right and left wall, there are open doors. The curtains are lowered on the doors. There are no locks on the door, only thick curtains. These doors are plentiful to the left and right of the straight path.

A caller calls at the beginning of the path: O slave of Allah, enter the path and do not deviate!

And a caller calls in the middle of the path: O slave of Allah, do not open the door! If you open it, you will nter it!

The Prophet (peace and blessings of Allah be upon him) explained this example: *'As for the way, it is Islam. As for the two walls, they are the limits of Allah. As for the doors, they are the prohibition of Allah. As for the caller, from the beginning of the path, it is the Book of Allah. As for the one who calls from the middle of the path, it is the admonition of Allah in the heart of every Muslim.'*

There are many avenues of evil today that were not present before. We should recognize the dangers of the Internet and cell phones and use them carefully. Many individuals enter into these paths of evil and are put in a difficult situation, especially the male and female Muslim youth. They are exposed to situations that relate to false ideologies, desires, doubts and other forms of evil.

Purification of the soul and keeping it away from harm becomes difficult if a path of evil is opened and a person enters the sinful path. A person should be very careful to protect his soul from desires and doubts when using the mobile phone or the Internet.

Allah says in the Qur'an: *'Tell the believing servants to lower their gaze (from looking at forbidden things) and protect their private parts (from illicit sexual acts). It's cleaner for them. Indeed, Allah is All-Knowing of what they do'.*

Most of the evil that reaches the heart and makes it sick and removes it from purification is by seeing and hearing something on the mobile phone or the Internet.

Heart diseases

All diseases have remedies. The Prophet (peace and blessings of Allah be upon him) said, 'Allah did not send down a disease from the sky except that He sent its cure'.

To know if you suffer from heart disease, you should ask yourself what is your defining characteristic? What is your defining character? How do others describe you? Are you known as a generous person or a humble person? Or are you known as an arrogant person or a hot-tempered person? As a Muslim, you should try to develop good traits and characteristics. If you have a bad trait, this could be due to heart disease.

It is mandatory to get treatment for heart disease. The spiritual heart is the most important part of our soul. When the heart is pure, the soul is pure. The root of all heart disease is the hardness of the heart.

When a person has a hard heart, he does not care about his relationship with Allah. He is unable to enjoy the acts of worship. Even if he worships, it becomes a routine without any enjoyment. He does not benefit from advice and has no motivation to attend a religious gathering or listen to an Islamic scholar. He usually commits sins without feeling guilty after sinning.

Hardness of heart is due to avoidance or minimal remembrance of Allah. Not feeling bad after committing a sin causes hardness of heart.

Following the desires of the body by overfeeding the body and neglecting the soul hardens the heart. Too much entertainment hardens the heart.

A man complained to the Prophet that his heart is becoming hard. The Prophet (peace and blessings of Allah be upon him) said, *'Caress the head of an orphan'*. Kindness to the poor and helping the needy will soften the heart.

Disease of Anger

The word *'ghadab'* means anger. No one is free from anger. Not all types of anger are blameworthy and some types of anger are not considered a disease.

Anger is sometimes praiseworthy when used for the sake of Allah without losing your ability to think and act according to Islam. But they are certain types of anger that are sinful since these make a person do sinful actions when he is angry. To purify our soul we should treat these blameworthy types of anger and avoid getting angry.

Blaming anger is excessive anger that causes a person to lose their ability to think normally. This type of anger can overtake a person's intellect and religion. When a person suffers from this disease of anger, he does not know what he says and what he does when he is angry.

The Prophet (peace and blessings of Allah be upon him) advised many who asked him for advice by saying: *'Do not get angry'*.

The Prophet advised us to control our anger. We can get mad, irritated or angry, but we should always be in control. We should avoid the bad consequences of anger if we intend to keep our souls pure. We should not allow our anger to make us do something that is forbidden in Islam.

First of all, when a person suffers from extreme anger, he should remember Allah and this should make him fear Allah. He will then become alert and aware of what he does or says because of anger. He should realize that he is a worshiper of Allah and wants to please Him. He should realize that if he behaves inappropriately, Allah will not be pleased with him.

The person suffering from excessive anger should familiarize himself well with the virtues of forgiveness, forbearance and restraint of anger. So after knowing the virtues of forgiveness he should not get angry but forgive the person who made him angry. He should not fall into Satan's trap and avoid becoming extremely angry as this is a disease that will destroy his soul.

He should realize that his anger is caused by the decree of Allah and nothing happens except by the will of Allah. He should be content with what Allah has decreed for him and should not be angry. He should also remember that excessive anger will lead to actions of which he will be ashamed. He should not injure his soul with extreme anger. He should save himself from embarrassment by actions for which he will have to apologize later, when he is no longer angry but ashamed.

He should know that people avoid those who suffer from extreme anger and they stay away from such a person. He will lose his family, friends and job if he continues to suffer from extreme anger.

He should seek refuge with Allah from Satan. If he stands when he is angry, then he must sit down. If the anger still does not leave him, then he must lie down. He should do wudu or ablution to calm himself. He should supplicate to Allah and ask Him to remove this evil quality of extreme anger and replace it with good qualities.

Disease of backbiting

Slander usually happens when the other person is not present. The person who slanders destroys his soul as this evil act can lead him to hell fire. Backbiting is talking about your brother or sister in a way that they don't like. Backbiting can even be done when the other person is present and you say something about them that they don't like.

We should protect our brother's honor and avoid violating him. The sin of slander is great in the sight of Allah. When you slander, you earn sin, which will blacken your heart and defile your soul.

Allah says in the Qur'an, *'Don't slander each other. Would one of you like to eat the flesh of his dead brother? You would hate it (so hate backbiting). And fear Allah. Indeed, Allah is the Forgiving and Accepting of Repentance, the Most Merciful.'*

You should think about your own mistakes and should not concentrate on other people's mistakes. We should make insignificant in our eyes the faults of others. You should be careful what you say and should control your tongue.

If you slander someone, you are actually harming yourself as you are the one who earns sins and punishment by doing this evil sin. You give up your good deeds when you slander someone. The person who slanders should realize that Allah always sees and hears him. We should speak in a way that is appropriate before Allah. We must not take our speech lightly and not say things that do not concern us. You should be in the company of righteous people who avoid backbiting and will discourage you from committing this sin.

One of our righteous predecessors said: '*Do not mention your brother in his absence except as you would love him to mention you in your absence*'.

We should make a strong decision never to slander.

We should not believe a person who tells us the bad things someone said about us.

The Prophet (peace and blessings of Allah be upon him) said: '*He who starts enmity between people by quoting their words to each other will not enter Paradise (even if they are true words)*'.

Allah condemned those who slander and those who did not stop the slander when it came to them.

Whoever spreads the news about people and stirs up enmity is the messenger of Satan and should not be believed.

Imam al-Hasan al-Basri (may Allah have mercy on him) said that such a person who comes to you and says, *'someone said such and such about you', will then go to another person and say that you said such and such about him. So don't entertain him. Think what he said is a lie. Ask him to stop as this is forbidden. Don't think of the person he defames as a bad person. Don't start spying to confirm or deny what he said. Just ignore what he said and move on with your life. Do not pass the slander and become part of the satanic train. Do not fill your heart with filth.'*

Disease – Hasad

It is obligatory for Muslims to remove heart diseases and purify their hearts from them. Envy (*hasad*) is a disease of the heart.

The person suffering from envy or *hasad* wants others to lose their blessings. Envy occurs when another gains power and authority. This person is so jealous of someone that he wishes him harm. He wants the blessings that make him jealous to be taken away from him. Envy is hatred and disliking the good condition of the envied. The envious person takes pleasure in removing the blessings from the envied person, even if this does not result in any benefit to him.

The Prophet (peace and blessings of Allah be upon him) said: *'There is no jealousy except in two cases: a person to whom Allah has given wisdom and he rules according to this and teaches it to the people, and a person to whom Allah has given wealth and property and with this he uses it in the cause of truth'.*

In another narration, the Prophet said that it is permissible to be jealous of a person to whom Allah has given the Qur'an and he recites it night and day, and a person to whom Allah has given wealth and property that he gives in the night and day.

In another narration, the wording of the Prophet is: *'There is no desirable form of jealousy except for two types: a person to whom Allah has given the Qur'an and he recites it day and night, so when a person hears him he says: If only I was given what he has been given, so I can act according to what this person is (upon). And a person to whom Allah has bestowed wealth and he spends in the cause of Truth, then a person says: If only I got what he got, so that I can act according to what this person is (upon)."*

Competition is healthy. It is considered praiseworthy when competing for justice.

Allah says in the Qur'an, *'Indeed the pious will be in joy. On thrones, watching. You will recognize the brightness of joy in their faces. They will be given to drink pure sealed wine. The last of it (that wine) will be the fragrance of musk, and let them compete who will compete.'* We should compete for our status in the hereafter and not for worldly things.

You may sometimes have envious thoughts, and it is not sinful if you do not act on them in speech or action. Whenever such a thought comes, you should immediately wish for your brother to have more of the blessings that caused you to have this envious thought.

The person suffering from envy should recognize that he is suffering from this disease. This is a dangerous and serious disease that harms the person. He is preoccupied with envy and this increases his hatred and having bad intentions towards the person he envies. He should instead be content with Allah's decree.

He should be satisfied with the blessings he has and also with what Allah has blessed others with. He should pray for the person he is envious of. He should ask Allah to give him and others more of what he feels jealous of. He should gift the person he is jealous of, and should give him something nice. He should treat envy with patience and be aware of Allah (*taqwa*).

The Prophet (peace and blessings of Allah be upon him) said: '*Do not envy each other, do not hate each other, do not oppose each other, and do not sever relations, rather be servants of Allah as brothers. It is not permissible for a Muslim to distance himself from his brother for more than three days, so that they meet and one ignores the other, and the best of them is the one who initiates the salam.*'

The Prophet (peace and blessings of Allah be upon him) said, 'By the One in whose hand is my soul, none of you believes until he loves for his brother what he loves for himself.'

We should cleanse our hearts of envy and pray for others to be blessed. To be Muslims we must be happy about what makes other Muslims happy and we must be sad about what makes our Muslim brothers sad.

Unfounded hatred for personal reasons and not for the sake of Allah is a disease of the heart. Muslims are brothers and sisters to each other. We may feel hurt sometimes, but we should never hold a grudge against our Muslim brothers and sisters for more than three days.

The disease Kibr (arrogance)

Kibr (arrogance and pride) is a trait of Satan. Iblis obeyed Allah because of his *kibr*. He thought that he is better than a human that Allah made from clay.

It is not fit for a human being to be arrogant as what we have is not our own but is a blessing from Allah. The earth we walk on was created by Allah. The air we breathe is created by Allah. The food we eat comes from the earth that Allah created. We make things with the intellect and the materials created by Allah. So how can we be arrogant? We are dependent and are very weak. We need the grace of Allah. We must not be arrogant and have pride.

We should sincerely repent if we are proud. We should accept our weaknesses and ask Allah to forgive us. We should know how small we really are.

Never think that you are on a higher level than others. Embrace others and be part of the people. Do the chores they do and serve them. Never think of a task as small and something that cannot be done by a person of high status like you.

Once Imam Malik (Allah have mercy on him) saw a man who was very drunk and foaming at the mouth but saying 'Allah' repeatedly. Imam Malik wiped the man's mouth and picked him and followed him home. Imam Malik saw a dream later in which someone told him, 'You have been purified as you have purified your brother'. The next day he saw the same man whom he had helped in the morning prayer. The man was reformed and he had purified himself because Imam Malik had been humble and kind to him. Imam Malik had come down to that person's level. He had given him dignity without any pride, so Allah purified and exalted Imam Malik.

If you help the poor and people in need, you have less chance to become proud and think that you are better than others. Also, do your chores as much as possible. The Prophet (peace and blessings of Allah be upon him) would take care of his clothes and shoes. He served others in a congregation and was not one to expect others to serve him. Many scholars used to go and clean the mosque and its toilet whenever someone praised them.

Think of how great Allah is and of His great creation of the Heavens and the Earth. You are nothing in front of them all. Remember that you will die one day and will be eaten by bugs when you are buried underground. You will be reduced to mere bones and will one day stand before Allah the same as everyone else.

Ghaflah (heedlessness): A disease of the heart

Ghaflah means indifference and forgetfulness. *Ghaflah* means forgetting Allah. Those who have this disease spend their lives thinking that they are not forgetting anything, but in fact they are forgetting Allah. So they are ignorant of their real condition. They may know Allah with their minds, but this learning has not reached their hearts.

To treat *Ghaflah* we should awaken our hearts to Allah and the reality of this world. Remembering death awakens the heart and makes a person come out of the state of *Ghaflah*. Seeing the graves can change the perspective and remove a person from *Ghaflah*.

A person should develop *taqwa* and become aware of Allah. *Taqwa* is a higher state of consciousness. Ask Allah to remove the *Ghaflah* and make you aware of the reality. Try to wake up regularly at night to pray. The person who has *Ghaflah* should try to be in the company of righteous people who often remind him of Allah. He should engage in remembrance of Allah.

Disease - Excessive love of this world

The Prophet (peace and blessings of Allah be upon him) said: *'Be in this world as if you were a stranger or a traveller.'*

We should be like the one who is not in his fixed abode and does not want to settle down in this world. We should be like a traveler who spends no more than required. He will not carry excess baggage when he travels as this would become a burden.

When we travel we only take a few outfits and the bare minimum. The same should be our attitude towards worldly possessions. We are travelers in this world and we should work on what we can take back to our final home in the hereafter. We should not collect the worldly things that do not benefit us in the Hereafter.

We should become aware of the reality of this world and its temporary nature. We should realize the true value of this world and how insignificant it is to Allah. Remembrance of Allah and association with the righteous company will help us to cure the excessive love of this worldly life. We should help those who are below us in terms of worldly possessions to know the reality of worldly life.

Step 3: Doing good deeds and improving our character

Obligatory actions

The Prophet (peace and blessings of Allah be upon him) said: '*The faith of a servant is not corrected until his heart is corrected, and his heart is not corrected until his tongue is corrected, and the man whose neighbor does not feel safe from his harm shall not enter Paradise.*'

The actions are the manifestation of what is in the heart. If the actions are corrupt, then the heart is corrupt. If the actions are righteous and good, then the heart is probably good.

We should perform the obligatory acts as these are the most beloved to Allah. To get even closer to Allah after the obligatory acts, we should perform the optional voluntary acts. The obligatory duties are like the roots of a tree and the voluntary actions are its branches. You cannot have the branches without first strengthening the root. The Mandatory Actions are the most important action you can take to cleanse yourself. Righteous actions are a cure for heart disease.

A sincere intention, love for Allah and His Messenger, trust and confidence in Allah and fear of Allah are some of the obligatory actions of the heart. To purify your heart, you should not have pride, arrogance, envy, greed and unlawful hatred.

The obligatory acts of the body are the ritual pillars of Islam - the daily prayers, obligatory charity, fasting in the month of Ramadan and the pilgrimage. These are the roots of the tree of action and are the most beloved actions of Allah. Don't underestimate them and don't go out looking to do other actions without doing these mandatory actions. Nothing brings you closer to Allah than these ritual acts. These are the essential actions for the purification of the soul.

Besides these important pillars of Islam, there are many other obligatory actions. Being dutiful to one's parents, fulfilling the rights of neighbors and maintaining trust are some of them. You should educate yourself about all these obligatory acts and perform them according to the Qur'an and Sunnah to purify yourself.

Avoiding the actions that Allah has forbidden is also obligatory. Purification will not take place unless you forsake the evil deeds. Among the evil deeds, it is most important that you avoid the major sins.

We should do righteous deeds willingly. The obligatory acts are a mercy and blessing for Muslims. We get closer to Allah and become better people when we do them. They are the basis and roots of our actions.

The Prophet informed us that the most beloved action to Allah is prayer at its proper time. After this act, the next act that Allah loves is to be just to your parents.

Prayer is the pillar of Islam. It is the pinnacle of good works and the pinnacle of obedience. Prayers not only increase our good deeds but also remove our sins.

The Prophet informed us that Allah wipes away our sins with our five daily prayers. Prayers are most important in the purification of the soul and the purification of the heart. The regular prayers remind us of Allah and our purpose in life. You should be alert and attentive in your prayers. Try to be in the mosque as much as possible. The quality of your prayer in the congregation is much greater than the quality in the house.

You should concentrate on the night prayer (*Qiyam Al-Layl*). Allah answers the prayers at this time (the last third of the night). You will purify your soul by doing this good deed regularly. Get up and cry before Allah.

Purifying your soul is a struggle. Try to stand up for the obligatory prayer in the first few months of the beginning of the purification of your soul. Try occasionally and later more often to wake up an hour before the Fajr prayer to pray the night prayer. This will be difficult at first, but will become easy after doing it a few times.

You should be detached from this world and excessive pleasures. Enjoy the good things that Allah has blessed you with, but in moderation. Live a simple easy life. Control your worldly desires for things and comfort in the hope of receiving something better in the hereafter. A simple life will help you purify your soul.

Your prayer must be of high quality. You should pray with attention, devotion and a sense of Allah's presence. You should pray like the Prophet (peace and blessings be upon him). Such an effective prayer will purify your soul.

Allah says in the Qur'an, *'And it (salah - prayer) is indeed something great (burdensome) except on the Khaashieen (those who are humble)'*.

Once you taste the sweetness of the prayer, it is no longer burdensome. So keep pushing and trying until you taste the sweetness of the prayer that cleanses your soul.

To make your prayers excellent, you should not jump into *Salah* (prayer) without preparing for it. Take a few moments to ponder and remember Allah and why you are praying. Then start praying, knowing that Allah is always watching over you. Your *Salah* is a conversation with Allah and you should not be distracted or go through the *salah* without interest in talking to Allah. Would you rush through when talking to someone you like (such as your friend), why would you rush through your conversation with Allah?

Allah says: *'My servant does not come near Me with anything but the obligatory actions'*.

Learn the basic meaning of all the words and *surahs* of the Qur'an that you say in your *Salah*. Be still when you pray. After praying, spend a few minutes in reflection and say the recommended words of remembrance and prayer. Do not stand up immediately after praying.

Zakah comes from the same root as the word 'tazkiyah' which means purification of the soul. Giving obligatory charity will purify your wealth and soul. It will increase your good deeds. Zakah is mentioned along with prayers in many places in the Qur'an. This shows its importance.

Zakah cures the diseases of miserliness and stinginess. People always want more and more. Zakah cures greed and makes the person satisfied with what he has. It increases the love in your heart for your brothers in Islam. The fact that Allah blessed you with wealth should make you thank Allah and be grateful to Him. This should humble you to know that there are many hungry and poor people in this world and you could have been one of them if Allah had willed. But Allah blessed you and therefore you should share the wealth with which Allah blessed you.

You should learn more about Zakah and its various Islamic rulings. You should give it secretly while being humble. Look for the best receiver for your Zakah – the righteous one. Give it to those who need it but don't ask. Give it to the nearest of your relatives who are needy and require Zakah. In addition to fulfilling Zakah, you maintain the ties of kinship when you give Zakah to your poor relatives.

Fasting makes you aware of Allah – develops *taqwa* (God-consciousness). Fasting draws you closer to Allah. It is a source of forgiveness for your sins. You should fast with a sense of happiness for having been blessed with the opportunity to perform this great act of worship. Fasting makes you realize the presence of Allah all the time. You do not eat or drink for only one reason - Allah is watching over you and He has forbidden them at the time of fasting. This develops your taqwa which helps you avoid sins during the year. This purifies your soul and keeps your heart clean of sins. You avoid committing sins as you realize that Allah has forbidden them and He is always watching what you do.

The Prophet (peace and blessings of Allah be upon him) said, *'For whoever guarantees to me what is between his jawbones and what is between his legs, I guarantee Paradise for him.'*

If a person can control his mouth and private parts when he fasts, he will be able to control them for the rest of the year. With their control he will also be able to control other sources of evil which cause the darkness of the heart.

Unfortunately, if we do not take full advantage of Ramadan, we will come under the supplication of the angel Jibril, who prayed to Allah against the person who is not forgiven for his sins, even though Ramadan came and went. The Prophet said 'Ameen' to this Dua (prayer) from Jibril.

We should be like the Companions who used to get excited six months before Ramadan and plan and wait anxiously for it. You should start preparing for Ramadan very early and many days before it starts.

We should purify our hearts by being generous and giving charity. We should do more good deeds in Ramadan. We should recite more Quran.

During the **pilgrimage** we combine the various acts of worship and get their benefits that purify our souls. We pray, sacrifice an animal and give charity. We give up everything during Haj for the sake of Allah and submit completely to Him. The physical pilgrimage purifies our hearts, removes the evil effects of sins and purifies our souls, leading to spiritual pilgrimage to Allah. After Haj, a person should change and become a better person for the rest of his life.

Voluntary Actions

If you only perform obligatory actions correctly, you will reach a high level of spiritual purification. You will be successful if you perform the mandatory actions correctly. But for most of us there will be a deficiency in our obligatory actions, and to correct them we have to compensate them with voluntary actions.

The voluntary actions will cleanse your heart from the sin of forbidden actions that you may have performed. So along with fulfilling the obligatory acts you should refrain from the forbidden acts to purify your heart.

When you perform mandatory actions regularly, you will want to perform many voluntary actions. This is natural. When you do one good deed, you want to do many good deeds. Good attracts good. So your actions don't just stop at the mandatory actions, but you will perform many voluntary actions. You will love to perform more purifying actions and you will want to get even closer to Allah with your voluntary actions.

There are many voluntary commendable acts you can do. Some of them are more praiseworthy than others. The Prophet emphasized some of the voluntary deeds compared to others and these are much more virtuous. We should first try to do the voluntary actions which are more virtuous and then do the less virtuous actions.

Only after performing all the mandatory actions should one consider performing voluntary actions. A person performs obligatory acts to fulfill Allah's command and to escape His punishment. But a person performs voluntary actions only to demonstrate his love, sincerity and true willingness to please Allah. He does not do voluntary actions to escape any punishment as this is not something that had to be done. He does voluntary acts only to get closer to Allah and to further purify his soul. He is loved by Allah when he performs voluntary acts as he does more than the minimum.

A person may be attracted to one voluntary act more than others. This is natural, but you should try to do all good actions. A person may love to offer voluntary prayers. Another person is prone to fasting. Some love to give voluntary charity and others love to make the voluntary pilgrimage again and again. You should thank Allah for making your heart love these voluntary acts. All of them bring you closer to Allah when you are done after fulfilling your obligatory acts.

A person who is so involved in performing voluntary actions that he becomes deficient in his obligatory actions is a person deceived by Satan. There is no substitute for mandatory actions. Voluntary actions should be performed alongside mandatory actions and do not replace them. You should not stay up all night praying and then miss the obligatory morning prayer

(Fajr). Instead, stay up all night if you can, but pray the Fajr prayer as well.

We know which voluntary action is more virtuous than others through knowledge. You should read authentic Islamic books and learn from scholars to know more about the various actions and their rewards. You should learn about Tawheed (the correct belief in Allah), the various articles of faith, the obligatory acts and the voluntary acts. Only with knowledge and actions will you be able to purify yourself.

Allah says in the Qur'an, *'The true believers are those whose hearts tremble with fear when Allah's name is mentioned, and whose faith grows stronger when they listen to His revelations, and they put their trust in the Lord. Who establish Salah (prayer) and spend in charity from the sustenance which We have given them. They are the true believers; they will have exalted ranks with their Lord, forgiveness of their sins and honorable sustenance'.*

This verse explains the traits and characteristics that make a true believer who has purified his heart. If we want to be true believers, we need to seek these traits and perform these actions.

If we do not pray our *Salah* with focus regularly and if we are not at peace when we give out of wealth, it means that we need to further purify our hearts to become true believers.

Allah does not look at our body and our appearance. He looks at our hearts and our actions. Our actions are a reflection of what is in our hearts.

The Prophet (peace and blessings of Allah be upon him)said: 'Verily, Allah does not look at your looks or wealth, but rather at your hearts and deeds.'

Sadaqah (charity) extinguishes sins as water extinguishes fire and purifies the heart.

The good righteous deeds are judged by the conditions of our hearts and our intentions behind doing them. Allah inspects our hearts and He knows if they are truly righteous actions.

Asking Allah

Along with the voluntary actions, you should pray to Allah to guide you and help you purify your soul. Only when Allah wills will you succeed in purification. So you should constantly keep praying to Allah.

The key to the purification of the soul is prayer and supplication to Allah. Without a key we cannot enter. The key to purification is asking Allah to help us purify our souls. Without Allah's guidance and help we can never be purified. Prayer can make the corrupt soul clean.

The Prophet (peace and blessings of Allah be upon him) said: 'There is nothing nobler to Allah than prayer.'

Asking Allah is the key to all good in this life and the Hereafter. It opens the doors and the path to goodness and purification of the soul. So whoever wants to purify his soul should turn to Allah in prayer and should increase his prayer.

We should use the prayer that the Prophet said, *'O Allah, grant my soul its Taqwa. Clean it. You are the best of those who clean it. You are its Protector and Master'*.

The Prophet also used to plead and say, *'O changer of heart, keep my heart firm on your religion.'* You should be sure that purification of your soul can only be by the Will of Allah, and Allah is the One who purifies whom He wills.

Allah says in the Qur'an, *'And had it not been for Allah's Grace and His Mercy upon you, none of you would ever have been clean of sins. But Allah purifies whom He wills, and Allah is All-Hearing, All-Knowing'*.

Nothing softens the heart more than asking Allah to soften it. *Dua* (prayer) softens the heart and Allah is the one who softens the heart. We should sincerely ask Allah to soften our hearts.

Allah says in the Quran, *'Rely on me and I will answer you.'*

Allah says in the Qur'an: *'When they turned away, Allah turned away their hearts.'*

By being the first to turn away from Allah, that person became unworthy of guidance. It was not Allah who turned away first.

Allah says in the Qur'an that those who ask for guidance will be guided, *'Those who strive in Our way, We guide them to the various good paths'*.

If we make an effort to turn to Allah, He will guide us and purify our hearts.

We can use the prayer often used by the Prophet, *'O changer of heart, keep my heart steadfast on your religion.'*

Recite the Quran

You should read the Quran every day. After reading, you should reflect and consider what you read from the Qur'an. You should then act on what you read from the Qur'an.

The Prophet said: 'The best among you is he who learns the Qur'an and teaches it.'

The best person is also the person who has purified himself and he is the most pious and devout worshipper. So learning the Quran and teaching it to others will help you purify your soul. The Qur'an is the cure for heart disease and it contains perfect guidance.

Allah says in the Qur'an, *'It is a guidance and a healing for those who believe'.*

Knowledge from the Qur'an will benefit you only if you have *taqwa* (fear of Allah). You should have an inner desire in your soul to do what is right and refrain from what is wrong, knowing that Allah is watching over you. Just knowing what is right is not sufficient if you do not fear Allah and act on knowledge. Many non-Muslims know that smoking and alcohol are harmful to their bodies, but they do not want to leave them because they do not have taqwa. So for the Quran to purify your soul, you should act on it and pray to Allah to give you strength to act on beneficial knowledge.

The Qur'an is the source of purification.

Allah says in the Qur'an: *'Indeed, Allah granted the believers a great favor when He sent a Messenger among them who recited His Verses to them and purified them and taught them the Book and Al-Hikmah'*.

The Messengers purified others with the recitation of Allah's verses. The Quran is a book of guidance.

Allah says in the Qur'an: *'Verily, this Qur'an guides to that which is most just and right'*.

There is no other way of guidance in purifying the soul, correcting the soul, making it upright, curing it of its diseases and defects, except by taking guidance from the Qur'an. The more you take from the Quran, the more you will purify your soul and straighten your heart.

We should recite the Qur'an, reflect on it and then act upon it to purify our souls. Acting on the Qur'an is considered part of reciting the Qur'an. Reciting the Qur'an is not merely reading it, but includes acting upon it. To purify our soul we should follow the guidance of the Quran.

Remembrance of Allah

You should always remember Allah. There are various words of remembrance that you must learn and say with understanding, thoughtfulness and presence of heart.

Make sure you learn the words of remembrance that are authentic and were taught by the Prophet. Our Prophet (peace and blessings be upon him) taught us all the remembrances that are pleasing to Allah. There is no need to invent new words of remembrance. Such new words, which are not authentic, will not purify your soul. You should learn the prayers before performing an action such as prayer before eating and should always say these authentic prayers to purify yourself.

You should consider Allah's creation and Allah's names and attributes. Thinking about the fleeting nature of this life and your death will soften your heart and remind you of the hereafter. By considering these subjects you will avoid sins and do lots of good deeds. This will cleanse your soul and purify your heart.

If someone finds it difficult to perform acts of worship, he should continue to struggle and perform the obligatory acts without missing any of them. At first the acts of worship may be difficult and not pleasant, but if he continues to perform them, he will find peace and relaxation after a few days or months.

To purify the soul, you should perform actions that are loved by Allah, even if you do not like them at the moment. Later you will develop a fondness for them. You should also leave actions that you like if they are not liked by Allah.

Turning away from the remembrance of Allah destroys our hearts. Those who turn away from the remembrance of Allah will have a hard life.

No matter how much wealth they have, they will live in a state of inner stress and discomfort.

The hearts of the true believers tremble when they remember Allah. They start crying and crying and remembering Allah and how they have sinned against Him. They ask him for forgiveness. They are concerned about the condition of their hearts. Most of us do not experience all these feelings as our hearts have become hardened and this is a sign of damaged hearts. This damaged heart is something we cannot afford on the day of judgment. Our success on that day will depend on the purity of our hearts.

Allah says in the Qur'an: *'The Day when neither wealth nor children will benefit. Only those who come before Allah with a pure heart (will be saved)'.*

When a person gets irritated when reminded of Allah, then this is a sign of a sick heart.

There are many cures for heart disease. A person with a diseased heart should try all of them to soften his heart and make it healthy. He should remember Allah as often as possible with his heart and not only with his tongue. He should engage in gatherings of knowledge and learning about Allah and His Names and Attributes. He should establish a connection with the Qur'an and regularly ponder its meanings. He should uphold the obligatory duties of Islam and pray five times a day. He should increase his voluntary prayers and acts of worship. He should remember death to destroy the love of the worldly pleasures that make him sin. When he sins, he should seek forgiveness from Allah.

He should surround himself in the company of righteous people. He should regularly be in the company of authentic scholars. Visiting and helping the sick will soften his heart.

Good companions

Our companions help with our purification. If your friends also fear Allah and avoid sins, you are in good company. Therefore, in order to purify your soul, it is extremely important that you take only pious people as your closest and most intimate friends.

Avoid being with friends who call you towards sins.

Always attend lectures of scholars and be among them whenever possible.

When you marry, choose your spouse based on her religiosity and good character.

Evil thoughts are not harmful as long as you don't talk about them or act on them. You should immediately seek refuge with Allah from Satan when you get these thoughts. You should fight against these evil thoughts. And if you sin, you should immediately ask Allah to forgive you and repent.

Consider your actions and take them into account. Look at your shortcomings and think of the righteous actions that you could have done but didn't. In this way you will be prepared in the future to avoid sinful action and to do more good actions.

We should choose good and righteous people to be our companions. If the companion is good, this will help to purify the soul.

The Prophet (peace and blessings of Allah be upon him) said: *'A man is on the religion of his best friend, so let one of you look at whom he befriends.'*

So if you want to purify your soul, you have to choose righteous companions to help you do good and stay away from evil.

Having a company of ignorant and inconsiderate friends destroys our soul. Our hearts will die if we surround ourselves with the evil people who turn us away from the remembrance of Allah. We will regret this company of people who destroyed our relationship with Allah on the Day of Judgment. We should become free from such people while we are still alive to avoid this regret on the Day of Judgment. We should surround ourselves with those people who remind us of Allah and soften our hearts. Our friends should not be those who accept us as we are, but we should be friends with those who make us better.

Good properties

We must first cleanse our soul of evil qualities and treat heart diseases before adorning our soul with good qualities. Both of these are a must for cleansing the souls. They can also occur simultaneously. Purification of the heart will happen when we rid our souls of despicable attributes. After this we must adorn our hearts with righteous, pure and good qualities.

Purification is purifying the heart and then increasing its goodness by cultivating in it or by filling the heart with goodness, acts of worship, and pure and righteous actions. If you want to purify your soul, you must repent and renounce sins, because sins corrupt hearts and hide it from the light of guidance.

The Prophet (peace and blessings of Allah be upon him) said: 'I was sent only to perfect good character'.

The Prophet said: 'A person will surpass the level of one who always fasts and prays (at night) through good character'.

The Prophet said: 'There is nothing heavier in the scale on the Day of Judgment than good character'.

When the Prophet was asked about the things that get a person most into Paradise, he replied: 'Fear of Allah and good character'.

Sincerity

We should sincerely purify our hearts only to please Allah. If we perform an action for the wrong reason, we will not be rewarded by Allah and the action will not purify our heart. If the action is not done solely for Allah, it will be done in vain.

If you did great righteous deeds without the correct intention, they will not purify your heart. A small act of kindness done for the sake of Allah is greater than a great act done insincerely.

An act done without the correct intention (that is not with the intention to gain Allah's pleasure) may count against you on the Day of Judgment. It can break your heart and destroy your soul. Set your intention right at the beginning before you begin the act of worship.

After completing the action, we should ask Allah to accept the action and remove the shortcomings and overlook the shortcomings of the action.

Mind your own business

When we do not limit ourselves to the things that affect us, we can become suspicious and slander others. Suspicion can make a person curious and he spies to look for more details. We should mind our own business.

The Prophet (peace and blessings of Allah be upon him) said: 'Part of someone being a good Muslim is that he leaves alone that which does not concern him.' When you point a finger at someone, three fingers point back at you.

The Prophet (peace and blessings of Allah be upon him) said: 'When the slave sins, a black spot appears on his heart. If he repents, it is removed'.

By renouncing sin, the black stain is removed, and he can then see the light of guidance and purify his soul. So the first step is to repent of the sin that corrupts the heart and obscures the light of guidance. The second step is to strive to cultivate the heart with righteous deeds, obedience, and acts of worship. Purification is achieved only by removing evil and renouncing sins. After repentance, do righteous deeds to further purify your heart.

Can someone clean themselves 100%? No, that is not possible. No matter what we do, we will have our share of sins.

The Prophet (peace and blessings of Allah be upon him) said: "All the sons of Adam are in sin, and the best of those who commit sins are those who are consistent in repentance." Repentance means turning to Allah immediately when you sin.

The Prophet (peace and blessings be upon him) said, "When the believer stands on the Day of Judgment, ninety-nine scrolls of sins will be placed before him, and each one will reach the end of his sight. Allah will tell him to read, and he will read until he begins to change color and think it is over for him. Then Allah will stop him and say: 'O My servant, did you ask for My forgiveness?' He says 'yes.' The bad deeds begin to turn into good deeds until the person will say, 'O Allah, the angel forgot to write down some sins!'"

Ihsan

We are created from three different components.

The first and most noble of them is *Rooh* (the soul). This is from the unseen and we don't know much about the soul.

The second component is *Aql* or the intellect or the rational. It is by this component that Allah separated man from the rest of His creation.

The third component of the man is his body.

When these three components are put together, they form the being called *Insaan* or man.

Allah has linked the three components of *deen* (religion) with the three components of man. Deen is composed of Islam, Iman (faith) and Ihsan.

Allah created Iman – the inner belief system (belief in Allah, the angels, the books, the prophets, destiny and doomsday) for the benefit of the intellect.

Islam – the external actions (prayer, fasting, zakah and pilgrimage) benefit the body.

Ihsan – the purification of the soul and perfection is for the benefit of the soul.

Ihsan is the perfection of one's actions. *Ihsan* means 'doing something good'.

The Prophet (peace and blessings of Allah be upon him) explained *Ihsan* as the worship of Allah as if you see Him, and if you do not see Him, then knowing that He sees you.

We should make our actions good by being sincere in our actions. For actions to be accepted and good, they must have the right intention.

The lower level of *Ihsan* is knowing that Allah is watching over you. With this level of Ihsan, you worship and perform actions knowing that Allah sees you.

The higher level of *Ihsan* is when you worship Allah as if you see Him. You do not actually see Allah, but it is as if you see Him. You worship Allah by knowing the attributes of Allah. The more you gain knowledge of Allah's names and attributes, the more your level of *Ihsan* will increase.

In order to purify our souls and worship Allah with *Ihsan*, we should learn more about Allah's names and His attributes. This knowledge is extremely beneficial and will purify your soul. You should know the names of Allah and act according to those names. For example, when you see a mother showing mercy to her child, remember Allah's mercy, which is far greater than any human being.

To reach the level of excellence in *Ibadah* (worship) you should hasten to Allah as there is no time to waste.

Beware of saying 'I want' or 'I must'. Instead, say that I will immediately begin to perform excellent worship. Start learning to pray with *Khushu (mindfulness).* There are excellent books and lectures that will teach you how to say your prayer in the best way. Say your *Salah* (prayer) slowly and with presence of heart. Take the right steps, change your lifestyle for the better, and gradually improve the quality and quantity of your prayers.

Change is possible as long as you strive to improve and ask Allah to help you change.

Al-Ghazali (Allah have mercy on him) said: 'How can people claim that they cannot change? A bear can be tamed to be friendly. A falcon can go from being wild to being a guide. A dog can go from being an attacker to a friend'.

If an animal can change its character, it is a sign for us that we can also change for the better.

Repent now and don't wait.

Allah says in the Qur'an, *'And hasten to forgiveness from your Lord, and a paradise as wide as the heavens and the earth, prepared for the pious'*.

You should not waste the time that Allah has blessed you with.

The Prophet (peace and blessings of Allah be upon him) said: 'Take advantage of five before five: Your youth before your old age, your health before your sickness, your wealth before your poverty, your leisure before you become busy, and your life before your death.'

You must use your youth and free time. These are the best times to perform actions that please Allah.

You should not perform actions for a few days and then stop performing them. For an action to be excellent and loved by Allah, it should be consistent.

The Prophet said: 'The most beloved deeds to Allah are the consistent ones, even if they were few'.

For example, do not pray 8 units of night prayer starting one night and then interrupt the night prayer altogether. Instead, pray 2 units of night prayer every night for many nights, and when you are comfortable with 2 units, increase it to 4 units and so on. Gradually increase your good deeds and be consistent.

You should always look at people who are higher than you in Islam. Do not be satisfied with looking at those below you in Islam. Be hard on yourself for your sake.

The goal of purification is Ihsan. When you reach Ihsan, you reach the level where your soul is at peace with its Lord.

With the cleansing process, you consistently engage in cleansing yourself, fighting yourself, and trying to eradicate the destructive errors. You do all these actions with haste as if today is your last day on this earth. You worship Allah as if you can see Him, therefore you worship Him in an excellent and praiseworthy manner. You make an extra effort and work hard when you know you are being watched. The amount of effort you put into your worship is in accordance with how active you are in observing Allah's observance of you.

Step 4: Remembrance of death

Remembering death and our encounter with Allah will make us realize the importance of purification.

Allah says in the Qur'an, *'O you who believe! Fear Allah and keep your duty to Him. And let everyone look to what he has sent for tomorrow.'*

Based on this verse, you should hold yourself accountable and fear Allah.

The Prophet (peace and blessings of Allah be upon him) said: 'Remember frequently the destroyer of pleasure (death)'.

Death is the decisive criterion between the life of this world and the life of the Hereafter. It is the decisive criterion between the domicile of the actions and the place of compensation for the actions. Death comes suddenly and today may be the last day of your life.

Allah says in the Qur'an, *'No person knows what he will earn tomorrow, and no person knows in which country he will die.'*

We do not know where or when we will die. A person can hope to live for dozens of years, but he can die today, even if he is young. How many elders have death missed, but youth taken away? Because of this, it is a must that you always remember death as this will help you purify your soul.

A scholar said: 'If the memory of death left my heart, I fear my heart would be destroyed'.

The Companions (Allah be pleased with them) used to imagine themselves in Hell and the tortures of Hell that they would suffer if they did not purify themselves. They also imagined the blessings of heaven. Then they asked their souls, still imagining their state after death, 'O soul, which one do you want?'

Their soul said, 'I want to return to worldly life so that I can do righteous deeds.'

So they told their present soul, 'You are able to do whatever you want, so work (do righteous actions now)!'

Say to your soul: 'O soul, if I die, who will pray for me? Who will fast on my behalf? Who will give charity on my behalf? Who will repent on my behalf for my sins and shortcomings?'

The excessive love of Duniya (world and worldly things) destroys the heart and comes between us and Allah.

The Prophet (peace and blessings of Allah be upon him) said, 'Just as iron gets rusted by water, so do human hearts'. When the Companions asked how to get rid of this rust, the Prophet said: 'Remembering death often and recitation of the Qur'an (reading it to seek guidance and act upon it)'.

Ibn 'Umar (Allah be pleased with him) said: "I was with the Messenger of Allah (peace and blessings of Allah be upon him) and a man from the *Ansar* came to him and greeted the Prophet (peace and blessings of Allah be upon him) with *Salam.*

Then he asked: 'O Messenger of Allah, which of the believers is best?'

The Messenger of Allah (peace and blessings of Allah be upon him) said: 'He who has the best manners among them.'

He asked: 'Which of them (the believers) is wisest?'

The Prophet (peace and blessings of Allah be upon him) said: 'He who remembers death the most and prepares for it best. They are the smartest.'"

Do we want to be among these wise believers?

The Messenger of Allah (peace and blessings of Allah be upon him) said: "Remember more often the destroyer of pleasures - death."

When we remember our death, we will not be attached to this world and its temptations. This life is transitory. The Hereafter and Paradise are the actual permanent life that we should strive to achieve in this world.

Remembering our death makes us patient and gives us a balanced view of life. When we are sad and in difficult circumstances, the memory of death lessens our pain.

The difficulty we face now will reduce our sins and increase our good deeds in the Hereafter. This difficulty is nothing compared to the difficulty and pain of death. So because of the remembrance of death we will not become extremely depressed and full of despair in the face of difficulties. Instead, we will hope that this difficulty will end soon and will not last forever.

The Prophet Muhammad (peace and blessings of Allah be upon him) said: "Remember death often because this wipes out sins and makes you disregard this worldly life."

When our circumstances are good and we are well in this life, the remembrance of death will lead our hearts to thank Allah for His blessings, and we also ask Him to bless us in the Hereafter. Remembering death will not make us arrogant and careless when we are blessed with an easy life.

Allah says in the Qur'an, "...*Verily, the life of this world is nothing but a [transient] enjoyment, and verily, the Hereafter is the home that will remain forever.*"

The Prophet (peace and blessings of Allah be upon him) advised us to prepare for death and the Hereafter. He (peace and blessings of Allah be upon him) said: "Be in this world as a stranger or a wayfarer."

A believer considers himself a traveler in this world and regards this life as a temporary place where he has to stop, rest and collect the things necessary for his final destination. He who thinks of his death will take the necessary precautions, and he who is sure of the long road he has to travel prepares for it.

The Prophet (peace and blessings of Allah be upon him) said: "The Hour of Resurrection has approached, but the people have become more greedy for the life of the world and more distant from Allah."

The digger who prepared the grave of Shaikh Ibn Rajab (may Allah have mercy on him) said: "Shaikh Ibn Rajab came a few days before his death and said (to me), 'Dig my grave there,' and he pointed to an area. When I dug it out, he lowered himself into it and laid down and liked it and then said, 'This is good.' The Shaikh died after a few days and was buried in the grave which he had prepared before his death."

Ibn Rajab (may Allah have mercy on him) said: "It is not true that morning or evening comes upon a believer except that he is in a state of repentance. This is because he does not know when death may surprise him. [Will he die] in the morning or in the evening? Will his soul be taken when he performs an act of obedience or disobedience? So if in the morning or in the evening he is not in a state of repentance, he is in danger of meeting Allah without repenting, and thus be gathered together with the company of oppressors."

The intelligent is he who imagines his time of death and prepares for it.

When Habib al-Ajami woke up in the morning, he said to his wife: 'If I die today, let such and such be the one who washes me, and such and such be the ones who carry me.'

Al-Maroof Idrees (Allaah have mercy on him) said to a person: 'Pray the noon prayer with us!' He replied: 'If I pray the noon prayer with you, I will not pray the afternoon prayer with you.'

So al-Maroof said: 'And it is as if you have hope that you will live to the afternoon prayer? I seek refuge with Allah from having long or distant hopes.'

When a person slandered another, al-Maroof said: 'Remember the cotton they will place on your eyes [at the time of death].'

It is reported that when Al-Hasan Al-Basri (Allaah have mercy on him) was on his deathbed, they asked him for advice.

He replied, "I will give you three pieces of advice, then leave me alone:

1. Be the most remote of people from the things you have been forbidden,

2. Be the nearest of men to do the good things you have been commanded to do,

3. And know that for every matter there are two steps you can take: one step in your favor (in the Hereafter) and one step against you. So be careful where you come from and where you are going."

Yahya Ibn Muadh (Allah be pleased with him) said: "I do not command you to give up life, but (ask you) to give up sins."

When Al-Hasan Al-Basri (Allaah have mercy on him) was asked: "Who will cry more than the others on the Day of Resurrection?"

He replied: "A man whom Allah blessed, but he used that (blessing) for disobedience to Allah."

Umar Ibn Al-Khattab (Allah be pleased with him) said: "Renunciation of worldly pleasure is a consolation for both the human heart and the body."

The pious and righteous people love this world only because it enables them to worship Allah and do good deeds.

Yahya Ibn Muadh (Allah be pleased with him) said: "How can I not love this life? Provision is enjoined on it by Him who keeps me alive and helps me to perform the deeds of obedience that will lead me to Paradise."

The righteous people are always prepared for death and do the things that they would do if they knew today was their last day.

Anas Ibn Ayyad (may Allah be pleased with him) said: "I saw Safwan Ibn Salim and had it been said to him: 'Tomorrow is the Day of Resurrection, he would not have had to perform an extra act of worship.' This means that he already did everything he could to succeed in the hereafter.

When death came upon [Abdullaah] Ibn Idrees (Allaah have mercy on him) his daughter wept. So he said, "Do not cry, O Daughter, for I have finished reciting the Qur'an in this house four thousand times."

No man can escape death. It is the ultimate reality that forces us to realize the worthlessness of pursuing the illicit pleasures of this world. Thinking about death makes us aware and we can then take actions such as doing good deeds to prepare ourselves for the eternal sojourn in the hereafter.

Hating death and ignoring this inevitable end of our lives will not be beneficial. We do not like to think about death as we think of it as an end to the worldly pleasures that we enjoy and the relationships that we value. But death is actually an entrance to the eternal joys of the hereafter, and only when we die will we have the opportunity to meet and see our Lord.

We should hope for Allah's mercy and generosity at the time of our death. We should seek Allah's forgiveness.

The Prophet (peace and blessings of Allah be upon him) said: "Let none of you die except while expecting good from Allah. Indeed, there are people whose expectation of evil from Allah has brought them to ruin and made them the losers."

A Muslim should have both hope and fear. We hope that Allah will show us mercy and forgiveness.

When we are healthy, we should prioritize fear (of Hell and Allah's wrath) more and therefore should avoid sins and do more good deeds. But when death approaches us, we should give more priority to hope (hoping that Allah will forgive us and bless us with paradise), and we should trust and submit to Allah.

When death was mentioned - Umar bin Abdul-Azeez (Allah have mercy on him) trembled and wept until his tears wet his beard.

Abdullah Ibn Al-Mubarak (Allah have mercy on him) said: "O man! Prepare for the Hereafter.

Obey Allah as much as you need Him, and anger Him as much as you can be patient in Hell."

Allah says in the Qur'an: *"Say (to them): 'Indeed, the death from which you flee will surely meet you, then you will be sent back to (Allah), the All-Knower of the Unseen and the Seen, and He will tell you what you used to do."*

Uthman b. Affan (Allah be pleased with him) said, "O people! Fear Allah and obey Him, for piety is a valuable prize. The most intelligent person is indeed the one who takes care of himself and works for it - towards that which comes after death, and through Allah's light (guidance) obtains a light for the darkness of the grave."

The intelligent person is the one who evaluates himself by his shortcomings in religion and works for the afterlife. He hastens to do righteous deeds before the chance to do them ends with his death.

Each passing moment brings us closer to our end. Every man must face death and taste its bitterness.

Allah says in the Qur'an: *"Every soul will taste death. And only on the Day of Resurrection will you get your full compensation. He who is removed from the Fire and admitted to Paradise has certainly achieved success. And what is the life of this world but from enjoying the delusion."*

Abdullah bin Shamit (Allah have mercy on him) said, "O you who are deceived by your long period of health, have you not heard of a person who died without suffering any disease (before death)? O you who are deceived of your long hope, have you not seen a person suddenly taken away (due to sudden death)? Are you deceived by (your) good health? Does it make you feel secure (from impending death) to have long hopes? Is it the Angel of Death that you challenge?"

We cannot hide from death.

Allah says in the Qur'an: *"Wherever you are, death will overtake you, even if you were in highly elevated fortresses."*

At the appointed time of our death, no one can prevent our soul from leaving our body.

Allah says in the Qur'an: *"Say: Verily, the death from which you flee will meet you; then you will be returned to the One who knows both the unseen and the witnessed worlds, and he will tell you what you have done."*

Hasan Al-Basri (Allah have mercy on him) said: "How strange it is that a people whose departure (from this world to the next) has been announced and whose ancestors have already departed are still playing around!"

We should therefore get busy getting ready and ready for death.

Allah says in the Qur'an: *"O you who believe! Do not let your property or your children divert you from the remembrance of Allah; whoever does that, they are losers. And use what We have given you before death comes to one of you and he says: 'My Lord! If only You would delay me for a little while, then I should give sadaqah (charity) and be among the righteous.' But Allah postpones no soul when its appointed period arrives. Allah is well aware of all that you do."*

This life is a test and nothing more. We should only take from it what we need for our next life.

Allah says in the Qur'an: *"He Who created death and life, that He may test you as to which of you is best in deed. And He is the Almighty, the Forgiving."*

Ali Ibn Abi Talib wrote to Abdullah Ibn Abbas (Allah be pleased with them), "Man feels sad for missing what he can never have and happy for what he can never miss (all that, that gets or misses is due to its fate). So be happy for what you have gained of the benefits of the Hereafter and sorry for what you have missed of them. Do not feel happy for what you have gained of the worldly benefits and be concerned about what will come after (your) death."

Don't be fooled by your youthfulness and health. The death of others before you was only to remind you of your own death. We are attached to this world and our houses. No one can settle down in his grave without first being removed from his house! Even kings are buried outside their palaces! You can't stay forever in the houses you built.

Ibn Jawzi (Allah have mercy on him) said: "How can the heart sleep peacefully while it does not yet know whether it will dwell in hell or heaven?"

We must repent and be better before we die. Doing so after death will not be beneficial.

When *Firawn* (Pharoah) saw that he was going to drown and die, he repented. But this did not benefit him because it benefits no one to believe and become a Muslim at the time when the soul witnesses the reality of death. The time to start doing good deeds and avoiding the forbidden is now. You should not delay it even for a moment.

Al-Hafidh Ibn Hajr said: "Extensive hope (of this worldly life) gives rise to lethargy when it comes to acts of obedience, procrastination with repentance, lust for worldly things, forgetfulness of the Hereafter and hardness of heart. The softness of the heart and its purity arises only by remembering death, the grave, reward and punishment, and the horrors of the Hereafter. If one remembers death, he will strive to perform acts of obedience. By remembering death, his worries subside and he is satisfied with less."

Once the Prophet (peace and blessings be upon him) passed by a group of people gathered around something. He (peace and blessings of Allah be upon him) asked: "Over what are these people gathered?"

He was told, "It is a grave they are digging."

Hearing this, he (peace and blessings be upon him) hastened ahead of his companions until he reached the grave. Then he knelt down and wept, and his tears fell to the ground.

He (peace and blessings of Allah be upon him) then turned to his companions and said: "O my brothers, prepare yourselves for a day like this."

The beneficial effect of remembrance of death is that it makes a person disregard this temporary life and makes him worry about the permanent life of the Hereafter.

Al-Daqqaq said: "He who often remembers death is blessed with three things - early repentance, inner contentment and attentive worship. He who forgets death suffers three consequences - delayed repentance, discontent and mindless worship." So thinking about death, its horrors, its agonies and its pains is really beneficial to us.

Remembering death before performing an act of worship will make us do it mindfully and with devotion.

The Prophet (peace and blessings of Allah be upon him) said: "Remember death in your prayer. Indeed, when a man remembers death in his prayer, he is inclined to complete his prayer. Pray the prayer of a man who does not expect to pray another prayer. And avoid any matter that would require an apology."

Death separates us from our family. It takes us away from our children and the wealth that we fought to achieve in this life. It isolates us from our friends who leave us when we die. Death moves us from the broad earth to the narrow grave. We will not own more than one chest. Our wealth will perish and our body will turn to dust.

Allah says in the Qur'an: *"But seek, with the (wealth) which Allah has bestowed upon you, the abode of the Hereafter..."*

A true believer seeks paradise in every blessing he gets in this worldly life. He spends his life doing things that will benefit him in the Hereafter instead of wronging others and oppressing them. Never forget that you will leave your wealth and fortune apart from your due share of the coffin. The purpose of life and death is to test who is good in conduct and deserving of paradise.

Remembering death controls our desires and curbs our greed.

The Prophet (peace and blessings of Allah be upon him) said, "Remember frequently the destroyer of pleasures - death. No one would remember it while it was close to life, but it would extend it to him, and no one would remember it while it was easy to live, but it would tighten it for him."

The grave is the first stop along the path to the afterlife.

Uthman (Allah be pleased with him) used to weep on seeing a grave until his tears wet his beard.

He was asked why he wept so much when he saw a grave, but not when he remembered paradise and hell.

He replied that he had heard the Prophet (peace and blessings of Allah be upon him) say: "Verily, the grave is the first of the abodes of the Hereafter. If a person passes safely through it, what follows will be easier; and if he does not pass surely through it, what follows will be more terrible. And I never saw a terrible sight, but that the grave is still more terrible."

The length of our lives is predetermined. We will all return to Allah at the appointed time. Our homecoming journey starts from the day we are born. We are constantly moving towards our death since our birth. Every day that passes brings us closer to it.

Allah says in the Qur'an: *"No soul knows what it will earn tomorrow. No soul knows where it will die..."*

It is the grace of Allah that we do not know when we will die. Imagine if you knew you were going to die tomorrow. This would make you very sad, upset and depressed. You probably won't eat for a few days before your death. Allah does not want to cause you such immense pain.

Also, imagine if you knew your death was far away. This would make you relaxed and you would not be afraid of committing sins. You will delay your repentance. So not knowing when we die is by the grace of Allah.

Death is the most painful experience we will surely have. It is the most horrible event in everyone's life. We have no power or control over our death. It will not respond to our cries and prayers. We cannot prevent, resist or delay our death. Modern medicine or other treatment will not help. We are all helpless in the face of death.

The rich and the poor, the powerful and the weak, the young and the old must all die at their appointed time. No one can intercede on our behalf and stop our death or even postpone it for a second.

Prophet Dawood (peace be upon him) once saw a strange person in his house. He asked, "Who are you?"

The man replied, "I am the one who does not fear kings, does not accept bribes, and the gates of the castle could not be closed to me."

Prophet Dawood (peace be upon him) said: "You shall be the angel of death."

He said, "Yes."

Dawood asked, "Have you come to take me before I have prepared (for death)?"

The angel asked, "Where are your neighbors, relatives and friends?"

He (peace be upon him) replied: "All died."

The angel said: "Have you not taken them as examples of death and prepared yourself (for death)?"

Allah has appointed the Angel of Death to take our souls.

Allah says in the Qur'an, *"Say (O Muhammad), 'The Angel of Death entrusted to you will take you (i.e., your soul). Then to your Lord you will be returned.'"*

Other angels accompany the Angel of Death and help him.

Allah says in the Qur'an, *"When death comes to one of you, our messengers (the angels) take his soul, and they never neglect their duty. "*

Angels who assist the Angel of Death may be angels of mercy who care for the soul of a believer, or angels of punishment who are in charge for the soul of a criminal.

When you prepare for death and do righteous deeds, your death will also be easy. The Angel of Mercy's assistant comes to a believer along with the Angel of Death. They come at the time of death reassuringly. They tell him of his great rewards in Paradise. They tell him not to fear and ask him not to grieve over what he has left of his children, family or wealth as Allah will take care of them. These are the benefits of being aware of death all the time and living an Islamic life.

If someone does not prepare for death and lives his life carefree, his death will be difficult.

The assistants of punishment come to a non-believer along with the Angel of Death. They come cruelly and frighteningly. They rip out his soul and beat him as they do so. They do not give him glad tidings, but frighten him by informing him of the Fire and of Allah's displeasure. They tell him of the punishment that awaits him because of his arrogant rejection of the truth.

Abdullah Ibn Umar (Allah be pleased with him) said: "The life of this world is paradise for an unbeliever and a prison for a believer. When a believer dies and leaves this world, he feels like a prisoner who was released to go freely on the spacious earth."

Al-Hasan (may Allah have mercy on him) said: "Beware of the perversions of this world, which are many. If a man opens one door to diversions, that door can open ten others."

We should stop rushing after this world and think about death, the grave and what comes after it.

The Prophet (peace and blessings of Allah be upon him) said: "Three things follow a person to his grave. Two of them return while one remains with him. His family, money and deeds follow him. His family and money return home, while his works remain with him."

Abdullah Ibn Ubaid Ibn Umair said: "Allah gives a tongue to the grave to speak with, and it will address a person and say: 'O son of Adam!

How have you forgotten me? Do you not know that I am the abode of decay, the abode of worms, the abode of solitude, and the abode of seclusion?'"

Step 5 – A cleaning program

Allah says in the Qur'an: *"In the alternation of night and day and in the creation of the heavens and the earth are signs for the people whose intellect is clear."*

To have a pure intellect, your mind should be free from anything other than Allah. Nothing should occupy your mind except Allah. Your mind should be focused and you should remember Allah standing, sitting and lying down.

To purify your soul, there should be a part of your day for solitude, seclusion and contemplation – a quiet place where you remember Allah. This should be the time when you think and consider.

Aishah (Allah be pleased with her) said: 'The beginning of the divine inspiration to the Apostle of Allah (peace and blessings be upon him) was in the form of good dreams that came true like bright daylight, and then the love of seclusion became bestowed upon him. He used to go into seclusion in the cave of *Hira*, where he used to worship (Allah alone) continuously for many days…'

The Prophet (peace and blessings of Allah be upon him) would go to Hira' for weeks. He wanted to think and contemplate.

'Umar b al-Khattab (Allah be pleased with him) said: "You should have a certain share of solitude, otherwise you will be indifferent."

Al-Hasan al-Basri (may Allah have mercy on him) said: "Contemplation is a mirror that shows you your good and bad deeds."

To cleanse your soul, sit and think about your situation and consider. Think about what Allah has commanded and how much of it you are doing in an excellent way.

Ibn Taymiyyah would meditate by the river bank every single day.

Imam al-Awza'i said: "At the time of the morning prayer or before it, the salaf would be as if birds were sitting on their heads, sitting and concentrating in worship, so much so that if a close friend came after being separated from them, they would not even notice it. After that they would meet each other and sit in circles. The first thing they will do is discuss the Hereafter. Then after that, they would discuss what would become of them in the hereafter. Then they would divide into other circles and study the Qur'an. Then they would divide into several circles and study the legal rulings until it reached the time of the afternoon prayer, and they would pray two units of prayer. They would then tell the jokes and sing the poetry of the time before Islam (which was clean without any bad stuff and they had their share of talking about the world)."

In the morning there should be time for solitude and thinking about your situation. When you take the time to think, you start to notice things.

Rabi'ah al-Adawiyyah says: "I have never heard the call to prayer, except that I remember the caller who will announce the Day of Resurrection. I never see the falling snow, except that I imagine the flying pages of the records of people's deeds on Judgment Day. When I see the swarms of locusts, I think of the great gathering at the last day."

Everything a person sees should remind him of the Hereafter and the Day of Judgment.

Imagine how much remembrance of Allah (by saying the authentic prayers and remembrances) you can get done on your way to work or on your way to class. The average person spends many years traveling before they die. Imagine that during this time of travel you did nothing but remember Allah.

Imam Ahmed said: "Once I traveled to al-Sham. When I reached there, I laid down to sleep in the mosque. Every time I lay down to sleep, the guard of the mosque came to me and told me that the mosque is closing, and that I had to go. I went out and slept in front of the mosque. The guard came out and picked up my legs and dragged me to the middle of the road. There was a baker who owned the shop opposite the mosque. The baker saw me and asked me to spend the night in his bakery. I went to his bakery and he made a comfortable place for me to lie down. He began to do his work. He took the dough and shaped it and put it in the oven. I saw him constantly saying, 'subhanAllah, alhamdulillah, la ilaha illa Allah, Allahu akbar.' I thought to myself that he didn't get tired. I stopped and asked him, 'How long have you been in this situation?' He said, 'What situation?' I said: 'Remembrance of Allah.' He said, 'I've been doing this for years.' Imam Ahmed said: 'And what have you seen as a result of your frequent remembrance?' He said, 'My prayers are always answered.' I said, 'You never asked for anything except Allah gave it to you?' He said, 'Except for one thing for which I am still waiting for the answer: to see Imam Ahmad.' I said, 'I am Ahmad!' I said, 'Allah brought me dragging by my feet to your bakery! Had you not prayed, I would have slept in the mosque."

Talk about Islam and purification of the soul with your family. Say "as-salamu 'alaykum" to each other. Hold family gatherings and remember Allah as a family together.

'Abdullah b. 'Umar narrates hundreds of words from his father, saying: "I heard my father say" or "I was sitting with my father when he said this."

Talk about Islam with your friends. Don't make talking about Islam unusual. Make it something ordinary.

Whenever two companions of the Prophet met, they would not depart without reciting Surat'al-'Asr from the Qur'an. Imagine if we had to do this with our friends. We should do this ourselves on the phone and recite this chapter of the Quran to each other.

The Prophet (peace and blessings of Allah be upon him) said, "If the time for a prescribed prayer (the five obligatory prayers) comes, and a Muslim performs ablution properly, (and then offers his prayer) with humility and bowing, it will be an expiation for his past sins, so long as he has not committed a major sin, and this is applicable to all times."

Allah said, *"Verily, prayer prohibits one from wrongdoing."*

Imagine feeling like your prayer was a conversation with Allah. Would you rush your prayer if you thought you were conversing with Allah? Give each of the five prayers their due.

Allah says in a narration of the Prophet, "My servant does not come close to Me with anything other than the mandatory actions."

Use the prayer to remind you of Allah. There is no way you can talk to Allah five times a day with piety and then commit sins. You will stop sinning naturally.

Al-Hasan al-Basri said that a person in the mosque should not look around before starting to pray. In the few minutes before you begin to pray, remember Allah.

Al-Hatim b. 'Asim (may Allah have mercy on him) was asked, "How do you achieve tranquility in your prayer? We see you so immersed. How do you reach that level?" He said: "Before I start, I imagine the *sirat* (bridge over Hellfire) in front of me. I imagine *Jannah* (Paradise) is to my right and Hellfire is to my left. I remember that whoever does not offer his prayers in this world will be caught by a hook on the *sirat* and will have to make them up in *Jahannam* (Hellfire). Then I imagine that the angel of death is behind me and I don't know when he will attack. Then I imagine that the Prophet (peace and blessings be upon him) is standing in front of me to monitor the correctness of my prayer. Then I remember that Allah, who created all that, is watching over me. Then I begin (to pray)."

Plan your daily schedule around your prayers. There are about twenty pages in each juz' (part) of the Qur'an. If you read two pages before and after each prayer, you will complete one juz' each day.

There are three categories of voluntary prayers:

1. The voluntary prayers which the Prophet (peace and blessings of Allah be upon him) never left.

The 2 rak'ahs (units of prayer) before fajr, 4 rak'ahs before zuhr, 4 rak'ahs after zuhr, 2 rak'ah after maghrib, 2 rak'ahs after 'isha'.

2. Recommended prayers which the Prophet (peace and blessings be upon him) did sometimes and left at other times.

Example: 4 units before 'asr – sometimes he did it and sometimes he didn't.

3. Pure voluntary prayers. These can be done anytime prayer is permitted.

The Prophet (peace and blessings of Allah be upon him) said: "On the Day of Judgment, the first thing you will be asked about is your prayer. If your prayer is deficient, Allah will ask for your voluntary prayers. Allah will patch up your obligatory prayers with your voluntary prayers."

You will then be asked about your obligatory fasts. The deficiencies are rectified with the voluntary fasting days.

If someone thinks that he cannot pray the voluntary night prayer in the last part of the night, then he can pray early in the night before he sleeps. The Prophet (peace and blessings of Allah be upon him) said: "Whoever of you fears that he cannot wake up in the last part of the night, he should pray before he sleeps. And whoever of you, who believes that he will be able to wake up in the latter part of the night, he should pray during the latter part as it is a blessed time."

Al-Hasan al-Basri was asked: "How is it that those who observe the voluntary night prayer are among the people with the most beautiful faces?"

To this he replied: "Because they commune with the Merciful, and He clothes them in light from His light."

Sufyan al-Thawri said: "Do not disobey him during the day and you will be able to worship him at night. I was forbidden to pray the voluntary night prayer for six months because of a sin I committed." The sins can keep you asleep.

A share of recitation and memorization of the Qur'an.

The Messenger of Allah (peace and blessings of Allah be upon him) said: "The best of you is the one who learns the Qur'an and teaches it."

Start memorizing the Quran. Set a daily goal to memorize a few verses. The chapter of the Qur'an you must read every night before sleeping is Surat'al-Mulk.

The Prophet (peace and blessings of Allah be upon him) said: "Whoever recites it every night will be protected from the punishment of the grave."

Daily and weekly charity

The Prophet (peace and blessings of Allah be upon him) said: "Charity is obligatory every day on every joint of a person."

Saying a kind word to someone and every step taken to pray the obligatory congregational prayer is considered charity. Guiding someone on the way is considered charity.

The Prophet (peace and blessings be upon him) said: "Every day the angels say: 'O Allah, reward the one who gave and withhold from the one who withheld.'"

The Messenger of Allah (peace and blessings of Allah be upon him) said: 'Whoever recites Surat'al-Kahf on Friday, a light will shine for him from beneath his feet to the clouds of heaven, which will shine for him on the Day of Resurrection, and he will be forgiven (his sins) between the two Fridays."

Fixed Mondays and Thursdays

The Prophet (peace and blessings of Allah be upon him) said: "The deeds are presented (to Allah) on Monday and Thursday, so I love that my deeds are presented while I am fasting."

Start fasting right after Ramadan when you are still in the habit.

The Prophet (peace and blessings of Allah be upon him) said: "There is an hour on Friday that if a servant calls upon Allah, he will certainly be answered."

Make sure to finish the Quran at least once a month.

The 6 days of Shawwal: Abu Ayyub (Allah be pleased with him) narrated that the Prophet (Allah's peace and blessings be upon him) said: "Whoever fasts Ramadan, then follows it with six from Shawwal, then it is (equal in reward) to fasting every day."

'Umar b. al-Khattab said: "Whoever has the means to go to Hajj but does not go to Hajj, let him die as a Jew or a Christian if he wishes." Make sure to go to Hajj if you can afford it and if it has become obligatory for you.

The way to get the angels to pray for you is for you to pray for your brother.

The Prophet (peace and blessings of Allah be upon him) said: "When you pray for your brother or sister behind his back, the angels say: '*Amin* - and the same for you." Pray for your brothers and sisters throughout the day.

Points for reflection and contemplation

In this chapter I will mention points, stories, proverbs and reminders that you can use for contemplation in addition to the daily contemplation of the verses of the Qur'an and the sayings of the Prophet (peace and blessings of Allah be upon him). You can consider one point each day.

- Your heart should be preoccupied with the love of Allah. The love of Allah should outweigh the love of all other things in it.

Allah says of the believers in the Qur'an: "He loves them and they love Him."

The Prophet (peace and blessings of Allah be upon him) said: "A man would not have attained faith until or unless he loves Allah and His Messenger more than anything else."

- The Messenger of Allah (peace and blessings of Allah be upon him) said: "Whoever eases the suffering of a brother from the sufferings of the world, Allah would ease his suffering from the sufferings of the Day of Resurrection, and whoever finds relief for one who is hard-pressed, Allah would make things easy for him in the Hereafter, and whoever hides (the mistakes) of a Muslim, Allah would hide his mistakes in the world and the Hereafter.

The Prophet Muhammad (peace and blessings of Allah be upon him) described Abu Bakr as-Siddiq (Allah be pleased with him), explaining to the people his status above the rest of them, he said: "He does not surpass you in performing more prayers and fasting - there are among you those who pray and fast more - but by something deeply embedded in his heart: *Iman* (faith) in his heart." Therein lay his superiority. There is no other faculty in the human body and existence that a believer should be more concerned about. We have to ensure that this faculty functions as Allah wants it to function and we should be very concerned about it. The Prophet (peace and blessings be upon him) used to pray this prayer often, beginning: "I seek refuge in You, O Allah, from the knowledge that does not benefit and from a heart that does not fear."

- Our bodies will one day return to earth, while our souls return to our creator. The medicine that Allah gave us to make our soul beautiful is daily obligatory prayers and optional prayers. If we do not take this medicine, our hearts and souls will be consumed. The condition of our hearts and souls at the time of death will remain with us for eternity. The only opportunity we get to purify our hearts is in this life, so we must take advantage of it.

- What does Allah do to purify us in this world? *Fitnah* – we are put through a test regarding our health or wealth or with sin. Allah sends us adversity and trials to purify us. At the end of *fitnah*, if a person is patient and does not complain or sin, then Allah exalts them so much that the Prophet (peace and blessings of Allah be upon him) said: "On the Day of Judgment, the people who were not tested will, see reward for those who were tested and wish they had scissors to cut their skins." Allah purifies us through tribulations such as the death of a loved one or financial difficulties. A woman came to the Prophet (peace and blessings of Allah be upon him) and told him that she had seizures and would sometimes be exposed. She asked that he pray for her and that Allah cure her of epilepsy. He (peace and blessings of Allah be upon him) said: "I can pray and you will be the same as everyone else, or be patient and you will get Paradise." She chose paradise and she asked him (peace and blessings of Allah be upon him) to pray for her so that she would not be exposed when she had a seizure. Through the hardships she suffered due to the disease, she was given the opportunity to go to paradise.

- There is no excuse not to cleanse yourself. You cannot give the excuse that you were born this way or that you are not from a Muslim family. Ibn al-Qayyim said: "Abu Talib drowned in the sea of error, while Salman the Persian was safe on the shore. Al-Walid b. al-Mughirah, the glory of the Arabs, preceded all in straying away from Allah, while Suhayb, the Roman, excelled above all Arabs. Al-Najashi was in Abyssinia and called Labbayk Allahumma Labbayk. Bilal (who was once) a slave cried out: 'Prayer is better than sleep.' Abu'l-Hakam (Abu Jahl) became deaf and became the father of ignorance. Another believed in Allah despite never seeing the Prophet. 'Abdullah b.Ubayy al-Salul prayed behind the Prophet (peace and blessings of Allah be upon him) for years and still died as an infidel."

Shaqiq Al-Bukhari (Allah have mercy on him) said to Hatim: "You have been with me for some time, what have you learned from me?" Hatim replied, "I have learned the following eight:

a) I have noticed that people used to preserve every valuable thing they possess. Then I reflected on the verse in the Qur'an: "Whatever you have will end, but what Allah has is lasting." So I decided to keep my valuables with Allah, the Most High.

b) I have observed that everyone has a loved one. but no beloved could follow the lover to the grave. Therefore, I have decided to love good deeds that would follow me to my grave.

c) I have reflected on the verse of the Glorious Qur'an which reads: *"And as for him who feared the position of his Lord and restrained the soul from [unlawful] inclination."* Therefore, I have made an effort to avoid desires until I have become accustomed to obeying Allah.

d) I have looked at people's concerns about property and authority. Then I pondered the words of Allah in the Glorious Qur'an: *"Verily, the most honored of you in the sight of Allah is (he who is) the most righteous of you."* Therefore I concerned myself with awareness and fear of Allah, The Most High, to gain glory in this world and the Hereafter.

e) I have noticed the spread of envy among people and reflected on the Qur'anic verse: "It is We who share their livelihood in the life of this world." Therefore I stayed away from envy.

f) I have observed the spread of enmity among people and then recited the Qur'anic verse: "Verily, Satan is an enemy to you: so treat him as an enemy." So I renounced their enmity and insisted on maintaining enmity against Satan.

g) I have looked at the humiliation of people in earning a living, and then pondered the Qur'anic verse: "There is no moving creature on earth but its sustenance depends on Allah." Therefore I occupied myself with performing the duties of Allah and put my trust in Him in earning a living.

h) I observed that people trust their trade, manufacture and health; I decided to trust only in Allah.

- Ibn Taymiyyah said: "Silence without reciting or remembering Allah or supplication to Allah is not worship, nor has it been commanded. It opens the doors to whispers (from Satan). So being engaged in remembering Allah is better than silence." Make sure that you remember Allah in the morning and the evening with the authentic Dhikr and Duas (prayers).

- Ibn Abbas (Allah be pleased with him) said: "Two units of prayer prayed with reflection is better than standing overnight in prayer with a reckless heart."

• Sufyan Ath-Thauri said: "Three among mankind will feel the greatest sorrow on the Day of Judgment. They are:

A man who had a slave, and on the Day of Judgment the slave produced better deeds than him.

A man who had wealth but did not give it to charity, but those who inherited it from him gave some of it to charity.

And a scholar who did not benefit from his knowledge, but taught others who benefited from it.

• Ibn al-Jawzee (Allaah have mercy on him) said: "You there! Sort out your religion as you sorted out your world - if your clothes were caught on a nail, you would take a few steps back to free yourself from it. Here is the persistent nail of sin that is stuck in your heart, if you took two steps back in regret, you would free yourself from it."

- An intelligent person said, "I am amazed at the person who mourns when he suffers loss in wealth but does not mourn the loss of his life. I am amazed at a person who sees his life in the present world disappearing, and his life in the hereafter approaches, yet occupies himself with the fading life and ignores the life to come."

- Al-Hasan said: "The example of the whole world, from the time it started until its end, is only a man who took a nap and then had a dream in which he saw something he liked - and then he woke up up."

- Shaikh Uthaimeen (Allaah have mercy on him) said, "When you are afflicted with a physical illness, you knock on the door of any doctor for a cure and are patient with any pain that you have to endure due to an operation [if it is necessary] and [you are also patient] with the bitter taste of the medicine [you take] – so why do you not do the same regarding the disease of your heart which was caused by sin?"

- Shaikh Uthaimeen, may Allah have mercy on him, said: "The more merciful someone is to people, the more merciful Allah will be to him - because you reap what you sow. One of the ways for a man's heart to soften towards the servants of Allah is that he is gentle to children and loving to orphans, for this will place a certain tenderness and mercy in it, and it is something that has been seen to happen."

- 'Ata narrates that there used to be a boy who used to go to the mother of the believers Aishah (Allah be pleased with her) to ask her questions and she would tell him. One day he came to her to ask her some questions. She said, "Son, have you practiced what you hear from me yet?" He replied, "No mother, I haven't." So she said, "Son, why do you seek to increase Allah's proof against us and you?!"

- The time to start practicing what we have learned is NOW!

Allah, we ask you to purify our souls and guide us to the right path.

Ameen.

www.ingramcontent.com/pod-product-compliance
Lightning Source LLC
Chambersburg PA
CBHW022133150726
47992CB00002B/572